REGANBOOKS

An *Imprint* of HarperCollins*Publishers*

THE DOUGHMAKERS COOKBOOK

125 Recipes
for Success in Baking
and Business

Diane Cuvelier and Bette LaPlante

WITH SAM STALL

Insert photographs and photographs on pages ii, vii, 75 by Alexandra Grablewski.
All other photographs courtesy of the authors.

HarperCollins books may be purchased for educational, business,
or sales promotional use. For information please write:
Special Markets Department, HarperCollins Publishers Inc.,
10 East 53rd Street, New York, NY 10022.

FIRST EDITION

Designed by Kate Nichols

Printed on acid-free paper

Library of Congress Cataloging-in-Publication Data

Cuvelier, Diane.
    The Doughmakers cookbook : 125 recipes for success in baking and business / Diane
Cuvelier and Bette LaPlante.—1st ed.
        p. cm.
    ISBN 0-06-056989-1
    1. Baking. 2. Doughmakers Gourmet Bakeware. I. LaPlante, Bette, 1953- II. Title.

TX763.C89 2004
641.8'15—dc22
                                                                                2003064089

04 05 06 07 08 WBC/RRD 10 9 8 7 6 5 4 3 2 1

For our parents,

Jean and Howard Cuvelier, who gave us the gift of family

Contents

Introduction

[*Bette*]

A couple of years ago I found myself on top of a mountain in the middle of the night, trapped in a furious snowstorm. As I sat there, terrified that the car I was riding in might plunge off a cliff at any moment, something occurred to me.

This was an awful lot of trouble to go through for bakeware.

This wasn't the first time that thought had crossed my mind. Here I was lost in the mountains, risking my life on behalf of the cookie sheets, jelly roll trays, and other products made by Doughmakers Gourmet Bakeware, a company I helped found. I was supposed to conduct a baking demonstration in Salt Lake City the next day, so our sales rep, Susie Talkington, and I had started driving there from Idaho earlier that evening. We'd been on the road for perhaps an hour when the snow began falling. Actually, "falling" is too mild a word for the blinding wall of white that surrounded us. I was raised in upstate New York, so I was no stranger to blizzards, but I'd never seen anything like this. Nor had I ever faced so much snow while trying to negotiate a two-lane mountain road.

And it didn't help that I'm afraid of heights.

Ironically, the snow actually kept my phobia under control. The white stuff fell so thickly that we couldn't see much of anything—not even the steep, terrifying drop that I knew loomed somewhere just to our right. Stopping was out of the question, so we crept along at five miles per hour, our heads stuck out the windows of Susie's Jeep, trying to make out what lay ahead. The only thing that prevented us from driving right off the mountain was the bank of tall weeds on the shoulder. Whenever we started into them, I'd say, ever so politely, "There are the weeds again. I think you have to go over that way."

This went on for miles. Susie nervously began singing hymns to herself. I started praying and repeatedly dialing my cell phone, which proved worthless in the mountains. I wanted desperately to call home, to say good-bye to my family.

Happily, that call wasn't necessary. After what seemed like ages, the snowfall eased and the road dipped down out of the Rockies. We made it safely to Salt Lake City. We were able to do the show, then soldier on to our next task in Provo.

And to the one after that, in Logan. And then the one after *that*.

On and on and on.

I can laugh about it now, but in retrospect it *was* an awful lot of trouble to go through for bakeware. And truth be told, that midwinter mountain passage wasn't the hardest thing I've ever done on behalf of Doughmakers—or even the scariest. But every escapade, every road trip, every unexpected difficulty has been worth it.

Why would I, and so many other people, attempt such things for the company? Because the truth is we *don't* do it for bakeware. We don't even do it just for profit. We do it for family.

Family ties are pretty much the only thing that could lure me, a dedicated homebody, into the Rocky Mountains or into the entrepreneurial world. Not long ago I was a suburban housewife with a husband and three kids, and no other ambitions beyond being the best mom I could be. But then fate stepped in. The scheme that would change my life, and the lives of so many others, first took root when my husband, Brooks, and I decided to help raise funds for a local Cub Scout pack. The idea was to have the kids sell some simple homemade aluminum cookie sheets. The plan succeeded beyond our wildest expectations. We started to look beyond fund-raising and realized we'd discovered a great business opportunity.

We took the plunge in December 1996. During a family holiday gathering my sisters, Diane and Barb, and I decided to start a company to make our own line of heavy-duty cookie sheets. We pledged our time, our fortunes, and our labor to what has become, in every sense of the word, a family enterprise.

Barb, who gave us essential encouragement and initial direction, eventually bowed out to help her husband, Chuck, start a photography studio. But Diane (whom you will hear from shortly) stayed for the long haul. While the decision to start a company changed my life, it utterly transformed my sister's. On the surface we couldn't be more different: me the homebody, Diane the self-confessed "wild child" who had been going her own way ever since moving out of our parents' house at age seventeen. Yet somehow, after plenty of soul-searching, we found common ground. In spite of occasional disagreements and a few full-blown arguments, we worked side by side for endless hours to turn Doughmakers into a reality.

Building up the company has been one big adventure, not to mention a lot of toil. All told, Diane and I drove some 350,000 miles during our first six years in business, hauling our wares to shows and state fairs across the United States. Then we convinced thousands of potential customers—one person at a time—that they could never do justice to their cakes, pies, and cookies without Doughmakers' help. As for the sheets themselves, during our first year in business the two of us made most of them ourselves, by hand.

All that effort paid off. Today Doughmakers products are sold in some two thousand stores nationwide. Instead of being made by hand, they're fabricated in a state-of-the-art, 50,000-square-foot factory.

Just as the company has grown and changed beyond all recognition, so have our lives. The Doughmakers saga is not just a business story, but a human story as well. It's the tale of two different-as-night-and-day sisters who turned a local fund-raising project into a multimillion-dollar enterprise. And it's about a dedicated group of employees and business associates who are eager to work for something more than a paycheck. They helped transform our rough-around-the-edges dream into a real company.

Our success can be seen in more than just the bottom line. We've built a company, but we've also built a family.

During our years of working together, we've learned lots about business, ourselves, and each other. My brothers, sisters, and in-laws have weathered financial and personal storms that would have torn other families apart. In the process we discovered how to conquer challenges we never in our lives imagined facing. Building a company taught us about self-reliance, bonding, and the value of friendship.

And it also gave us one heck of a story—plus tons of recipes—to share.

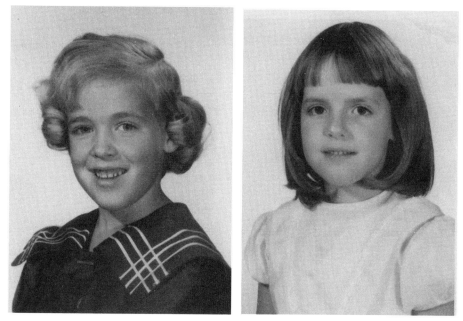

Bette   *Diane*

Our Story

Homemade
Memories

[*Bette*]

If you want to understand Doughmakers, you have to understand my family first. And if you want to understand my family, you have to come to dinner.

I was born in 1953 in Rochester, New York, the second oldest of Howard and Jean Cuvelier's seven children. Our extremely full house included my older sister, Barbara, then me, followed by Beverly, Clay, Diane, Donnie, and Richard. Not surprisingly, the Cuvelier household was one of the livelier spots in our neighborhood. It was loud. It was boisterous. And it was, for the most part, loads of fun.

During mealtimes our kitchen was as busy and often as crowded as a short-order restaurant. It was in these trial-by-fire surroundings that all my brothers and sisters and I learned how to bake cakes, fry eggs, boil spaghetti, and do all the other chores necessary to put a meal for nine on the table. Sunday dinners were the true test, because it was usually a complete, semiformal feast with all the trimmings. And because there were so many mouths to feed, even the smallest dishes were big deals. If you wanted, say, mashed potatoes with your roast beef, you had to peel ten pounds of spuds, then boil and mash them. So, needless to say, come Sunday if we weren't in church, we were in the kitchen helping out.

Bette (right), age 5, with sister Barb, age 6,
starting their baking careers by helping their mother.

When did I learn to cook? I really can't say. It probably wasn't too long after I learned to walk and talk. Really, I can't remember a time when I wasn't
measuring and mixing. That's probably why I had so little patience with people
my age who were helpless in front of a stove. We Cuveliers could *all* cook. In
the seventh grade I even made a full Thanksgiving dinner. Mom was in the
hospital, so I did the whole thing, from soup to nuts. Of course no one gave any
thought to the idea that I *couldn't* do it. Because I'd helped out in the kitchen
for so long, things like mixing the dressing (my favorite!) and basting the bird
were already second nature. Grandma Minnie was there, and I think I really
impressed her—partly with my cooking but mostly with my mastery of our new
automatic dishwasher. I remember her saying, as my fingers flew over the
washer's control panel, "I can't believe kids know how to do all this." I think I
pressed a few extra buttons just to show off.

Most day-to-day dinners weren't that elaborate, though they were still delicious. I remember that on our birthdays each of us kids got to pick the meal.
Mine was always spaghetti. My sister Barb's was macaroni and cheese. My sister
Beverly's was roast beef. But on regular days we saw a lot of casseroles plus
crowd pleasers such as chili con carne. I loved all of it. I remember thinking al-

most every day, "I wonder what we're having for dinner tonight?" I guess even then I was obsessed with food.

Our parents were obsessed with keeping us safe and healthy, though when it came to parenting styles, Mom and Dad were polar opposites. Dad, a soldier in World War II, then a career-long blue-collar worker for the Kodak company, played the role that fathers often did in those days. He provided the discipline when it was needed.

Mom was born the youngest of thirteen children. Her own mother died when she was one year old, so she and her next-oldest sister were adopted by two childless sisters and raised as cousins. She was brought up as an only child by her adoptive mother—my Grandma Minnie, who, as you will hear shortly, ran a very tight ship. Having been raised in such a strict household, Mom felt more inclined to let her kids have their own way.

She's as humble as she is easygoing. Showiness is almost a sin to her, as I learned when, after graduating from high school, I took her for a ride in the brand-new convertible I bought with money from my first real job as a hairdresser. At a stoplight we pulled up next to some friends of mine, and I told them in breathless detail about my ride. But as soon as they pulled away, Mom said, "Bette, you shouldn't brag." I felt so deflated. I mean, what good is having a new car if you can't talk about it? In retrospect, of course, I understand what she was telling me: It's okay to have nice things, just don't hurt other people's feeling by carrying on about them.

Mom loved us kids, but seven was a handful for her, as it would be for anybody. Even when I was a little kid, I used to worry about how she was holding up. In fact, I seemed prone to worrying in general. It was such an obvious trait that my nickname became "the little mother." I felt as if I needed to help Mom, to the point where I felt guilty going outside to play. Instead I would change diapers and feed the babies their bottles and try to be her helper. I hated to disappoint people, and I made a point of trying to give them what they wanted. Of course, this behavior is somewhat odd in an eight-year-old, but years later my we-aim-to-please attitude would serve me well in Doughmakers.

One of the other, more practical traits that all of us kids developed was a keen understanding of the value of a dollar—primarily from years of not having very many. Our dad wasn't poor by any means, but we certainly weren't rich, either. When he retired in 1979, we were shocked to learn that he'd supported a household of nine on $17,000 a year. He did "trick work" (you might know it as working the "swing shift") all his life. First he'd spend several weeks

Bette helping Grandma Minnie
with her daily chores.

on a more or less normal, eight-to-four schedule; then he'd move to a four-to-midnight shift and then to a midnight-to-eight shift. During the night and morning cycles he'd try to sleep during the day. With seven kids around, it wasn't easy. There was no air-conditioning in the house, so our windows were wide open during the summer. And of course every kid in the neighborhood liked to play at our place.

In spite of this, during the day Mom would frantically try to keep us quiet. "Shhh . . . your father's sleeping," she would say. Growing up I think my brothers, my sisters, and I must have heard that a thousand times.

Being around so many people so much of the time, we all learned that the world didn't revolve around our individual needs or concerns. I think that made us more flexible, more tolerant of last-minute changes, and better team players than the average bear. It also taught us to look out for one another. In a way we're sort of codependent. Our happiness depends on one another's well-being.

Which is, I think, exactly what our parents wanted. They let us know by their actions that blood was thicker than water and that the family would always be there for us. And even though Dad was strict, when the chips were down, he backed us up. Life at the Cuvelier house could be chaotic, it could be crazy, but there was love. Love and lots of food.

As I mentioned earlier, our kitchen skills far exceeded those of our peers. I remember being amazed that my grammar school friends couldn't fry eggs, and I was fascinated by one high school buddy, Kathy, who was lucky if she got out of the kitchen without burning whatever she was making. (She has since become an excellent cook in her own right.) She stayed over one weekend, and on Saturday morning she decided to make waffles with Diane (who was maybe eight at the time). I helped her increase the size of the recipe she found, but something got lost in the translation. Instead of making waffle batter, she created an incredibly strong adhesive. It sealed the waffle iron so tightly shut that we couldn't get it open—ever. We laugh over that story to this day, but Mom doesn't think it's funny. She's still upset over that waffle iron.

Of course, just because I knew my way around the stove didn't necessarily make me a gourmet. Although I spent my days helping to prepare full-course meals, my personal favorites as a small child were peanut butter with sugar, and raw potatoes with salt. Honestly. I used to mix this stuff up and then sit out by the garage and eat it. I remember thinking that when I grew up I would make it for my family every night. To their immense relief I never did. However, a few of those childhood quirks did sneak into my adult life. When I was first married, I only knew how to cook in large quantities—really, really large quantities. My husband, Brooks, would come home, look at all the pots on the stove,

Bette, in 1970,
helping prepare
Christmas dinner.

Grandma Minnie Baldwin with her first six grandchildren: (from left) Bette, Clay, Diane, Grandma, Donnie, Bev, and Barb. Number seven, Richard, was on the way.

and ask in all seriousness, "Who's coming over for dinner?" It's a good thing he didn't mind leftovers.

While my mom provided basic culinary training, you could say I got my master's degree from my maternal grandmother, Minnie Baldwin. We were regular visitors to her house in the small upstate New York town of Wellsville, and she to ours. We kids would go to her place each summer, two at a time, to spend a couple of weeks with her. Grandma Minnie made the most wonderful pies and cakes (you can find her recipe for Banana Cake with Whipped Cream Frosting on page 155, and for Date Nut Cake on page 156). When you opened the back door to her house, the smell of food surrounded you.

Her specialty—and the thing we kids enjoyed most—was breakfast. In the morning we would wake to the smell of it. We weren't normally too happy about getting up at 7 A.M. on Saturdays, but when you got a whiff of what was cooking in the kitchen, you made an exception. There were eggs, bacon, sausage—all our favorites. When the whole family visited, Grandma would actually set a toaster on an extra chair, right next to her at the table, so she could keep up with the demand for toast. And here's the really interesting part: We had *dessert* afterwards. That's right, no breakfast was complete unless it ended with cake or pie.

In retrospect, I wonder where we put it all. The centerpiece was another sweet item, her thin, almost crepe-like buttermilk pancakes. Unfortunately, I can't share the recipe. Grandma didn't measure anything; she just tossed ingredients in a bowl. But I think part of the secret was the pork sausage she purchased from a smokehouse in town. She used the grease not just on the griddle but in the pancakes themselves. It gave them a totally unique and totally delicious flavor. I can still remember that taste. As kids we would have contests to see who could eat the most (Bev could put away as many as thirty). It's such a shame that we'll never taste them again. When Grandma passed away in 1973, she took the secret with her.

Grandma's breakfasts were great, but her dinners were wonderful, too. When we went to visit, all seven of us kids plus Mom and Dad would gather around her gigantic dining room table. And all of us kids would have to wear aprons—not napkins but full aprons, both boys and girls. You couldn't pull up a chair without one. We got our first aprons as tiny children, and as the years passed and we grew, we didn't get new ones. Grandma Minnie just sewed extra material onto the apron bottoms. We four oldest kids wore our oft-mended models for more than a decade. And, of course, Grandma wore one pretty much all the time herself. There was a method, sort of, to her madness. Back then we washed clothes only once a week, so getting food or dirt on an otherwise perfectly clean garment seemed a terrible waste. And so, right up through high school, we wore aprons to Grandma's table.

Grandma wouldn't tolerate any lip, but sometimes her rules were kind of refreshing. We grew up in a house with lots and lots of freedom, so occasionally a little bit of structure (okay, a lot) was a relief. Looking back, I sometimes think we've given up too much of that discipline—for instance, eating together as a family. Back then it was a hard-and-fast rule. These days it's a minor miracle. Right now my own dining room table is serving as a family workstation of sorts. Dinner is either at the kitchen counter or, even worse, in front of the television.

Luckily, my brothers, sisters, and I still have our memories and each other. At Mom and Dad's house, filled with laughter and chaos and fun, I learned how to take care of myself and others, and how to keep my wits when everything around me dissolved into chaos. Best of all, I discovered the value of sticking together. And from Grandma Minnie I learned about discipline and perseverance and the importance of never settling for second best.

That, and how to bake an awesome apple pie.

Kid Stuff

[*Diane*]

In 1965, when I was six years old, I got an Easy Bake oven for Christmas. I thought it was the coolest present in the world. All that day I popped out cakes for my brothers and sisters. I'm sure I went through all the mixes right away. After that I started making up my own concoctions.

Frankly, I'm not sure why I found it so fascinating. At that age I didn't have to *play* at cooking. In fact, I remember making a real cake from scratch not too long afterwards. It was just a standard white cake with white icing, but I was certainly proud—even though I managed to coat the entire kitchen with flour while mixing the batter. In a big family like ours, whenever you could accomplish something and get credit for it, you felt as if you were queen for a day.

Like all the Cuvelier kids, I knew my way around the kitchen, but for me, learning to cook wasn't so much about helping out as it was about avoiding starvation. Meals could be a feeding frenzy, with me the littlest shark. The drill at dinner was (1) get there, (2) sit down, and (3) grab as much as you could and swallow fast.

It was a good thing I became self-sufficient, because I wasn't destined to stay in the nest for long. It seems as if from the time I could walk, I wanted to get out of the house. Mom can tell harrowing tales of how, even at a very young

Diane received an Easy Bake oven for Christmas when she was six. She used all the mixes that came with it the very first day.

age, I would sometimes simply disappear. Then, after a frantic search, I'd be apprehended blocks away, busy on some mission of exploration.

Bette and I are two very different people, in part because of nature, in part because of nurture. We grew up in the same house, surrounded by the same people, but because of our places in the birth order, we saw those childhood years from entirely different perspectives. While she was near the top looking down, I was near the bottom looking up. Bette was the second oldest and already had a well-established sense of herself before the rest of us started arriving. I came along in 1959. With four before me and two to follow, I felt lost in the middle.

Our family was so big that my parents ran out of baby names before they ran out of babies. When my very youngest brother was born, they let Barbara and Bette come up with his name. I kid you not. It just so happened that my sisters were madly in love with two brothers down the street, one named Richard, the other Steven. So I guess you could say the youngest in our family, Richard Steven Cuvelier, is a living memorial to those preteen crushes.

Richard, Donnie, and I were the "little kids." My parents had a very, very large dining room table, but if ever we had too many guests and not enough

Back row: Barb, Bette, Mom, C.J., Dad, and Bev. Front row: Richard, Diane, and Donnie.

chairs, we three would be stranded at the kiddie table. And while Bette was so concerned about helping Mom that her nickname was "the little mother," mine could easily have been "the little monster." In fact, I'd like to take this opportunity to apologize to my mother. She's the littlest slip of a woman, yet she worked like a horse to make sure we were fed and clothed and safe. And in return we—okay, mostly *I*—got into enough trouble to keep her in knots for most of my childhood.

If Dad was around, making waves was usually out of the question. If Mom was home alone, I was pretty much ready to wreak havoc. And if both of them left, there was no limit. Mom was a nurse, and during my early teenage years she worked a lot of evenings at a nursing home. Donnie, Rich, and I would be left by ourselves in the house. We considered this a golden opportunity to try to kill one another. I still have a scar on my right ring finger from the time Donnie and I fought over a pair of scissors. These days he's the sweetest person in the world, but back then for some reason he was my mortal enemy. Our house just wasn't big enough for the two of us—especially when there was no one else in it.

Not that Bette was perfect. She used to sneak into my parents' bedroom at night on hands and knees, creep up to the cedar chest at the end of the bed where Dad laid his pants, and dig around for spare change. And she was the *good* one. No wonder Mom seemed at wits' end so often.

Over the years I got better and better at staying out of the house. Pretty much any friend I had became a "Can I stay at your house tonight?" kind of friend as quickly as possible. By the fifth or sixth grade I had gotten close with one of my best childhood buddies, Jennifer. She taught me how to smoke. I developed a pack-a-day habit by age thirteen (which I didn't kick for another thirty years). And then I met Tori, who was involved in one of my weirder run-ins with authority—weird because it involved, of all things, baked goods. When we were about fourteen, we got in the habit of stealing boxes of Jell-O cheesecake mix from the local grocery store. It was easy to grab. All you had to do was open the box, remove the two mix packets, and jam them in your pockets. We'd steal some pretty much every day and then make the cheesecake. But

We thought the kids' table was the best place to be. Grandma and Grandpa gave us "our table" for Christmas.

My, how we've grown: Doughmakers' employees at our facility in Terre Haute, Indiana, June 2003.

one day, just as we were sneaking out of the store, we were caught and marched up to the office. The manager got our parents' names and tried to call them, but by some miracle he couldn't get hold of anybody. He thought we were giving him fake names and phone numbers, so he told us to produce some ID. We were only fourteen, so all we could show him were our Weight Watchers workshop cards—and here we were stealing cheesecake! The irony was too much for the poor man to process. I sensed he was about to wash his hands of the mess and cut us loose, but then he tried my house one last time. That sank us.

My parents had been outside, getting ready to go camping with the other kids, but my dad forgot something and ducked back in the house—just in time to hear the phone ring. Our "sentence" was for Tori and me to go along on that family campout. I was used to that sort of thing, but for Tori it was "hard time"—forty-eight hours in the woods without smoking, drinking, or, for the most part, cursing.

By age seventeen I was no longer trying to get away, I was gone. I moved out for good with Tori, my sister Bev, and one of my best friends, Cindy. Strangely enough, my relationship with my family improved after I left. Once I was making my own way in life, I think I could face them on a more equal footing. And although I experienced our home life differently from Bette, I took away many of the same life lessons she did, including how to fly by the seat of my pants and stay focused in chaotic situations. In fact, I think I actually work better under such conditions. If everything's easy, there's no challenge.

The best part is that all those family members I had so much trouble relating to became my best friends—even Donnie, especially Donnie. When we were little, he was the bane of my existence. The little rat would even blackmail me. Actually he'd blackmail anybody, but mostly me because I was the one he always seemed to catch. He had all kinds of dirt on me, and I was paying him off left and right—usually with cash I raided from Mom's purse.

A few years ago he finally got a chance to be on the receiving end. When he was getting married, I went out to dinner with Donnie, his fiancée, her sister, and our brother Rich. We sat at the restaurant telling horrible stories one after another about what a monster he'd been. Each one was more appalling and more unbelievable than the last.

Finally, Donnie's fiancée and her sister got up to use the bathroom. As soon as they were out of sight, Donnie leaned over and said, "I'm trying to marry this girl. Can you please stop saying these things?"

With total seriousness, I said, "What's it worth to you?"

I feel blessed that we all came to a place where we could understand and accept each other. I am even more blessed that we get to work together in this company we started. But we had to take some very different roads to get there. Bette will share her own story later. As for me, let's just say that while my professional life paralleled hers, emotionally our journeys couldn't have been more different.

During high school I took vocational classes in hairdressing. Then I quit and worked at a nursing home as an assistant for a while. After some not-so-gentle prodding from Bette, I went *back* to hairdressing; I learned the ropes at the Continental School of Beauty in downtown Rochester. I graduated with what amounted to a double major: styling and partying. I worked and partied in the Rochester area until 1980 when I decided to move with my sister Bev and her daughter, Jaimeé, to Florida. Mom and Dad had retired to the town of Spring Hill, near Tarpon Springs, so we settled in that area, too.

And then a lot of very bad things happened in a very short time. In 1982, just a day before I was supposed to go with my parents on their annual return trip to Rochester, Dad died of a heart attack. Shortly thereafter I married, briefly, and then divorced. Shortly after that I got into a ten-year relationship with the father of my two children: Emily (born in 1985) and Tommy Jr. (born in 1990). The relationship was doomed from the start. Let's just say that he was capable of the most insane, abusive jealousy and, yes, he drank like a fish. In our decade together he changed me from being the happy-go-lucky life of the party into someone who was afraid to mention a man's name in the house. Slowly but surely he chipped away at my self-esteem. I tried to leave him at least six times. But then things would get tough for me and the kids, and he'd call and say exactly the right stuff on the phone, and I'd go back. Things would be exactly as they were before except that each time they got a little worse.

Finally, in the spring of 1994, I packed and moved myself, Emily, and Tommy Jr., back to Rochester. Thanks largely to my daughter (who stated in no uncertain terms that she would never go back to her father), this time I made it stick. From there we moved to the California town of Redding, not far from where Bev had put down roots. But money was tight, rents were high, and good jobs few and far between. I'd gotten my kids out of a bad, go-nowhere relationship, and now I had to get myself out of a bad, go-nowhere professional life. But what could I do? Just then I caught a break. It was one of those opportunities that comes around only once . . . if you're lucky.

One day in the early winter of 1996, Barb called to tell me that Bette and Brooks had bought some plane tickets for us, and they wanted the kids and me to fly to their house in Terre Haute, Indiana, for a Christmas family reunion. And there was something else, too.

"Bette and Brooks have been talking to me about starting some sort of business with them," Barb said. "I think you should get in on it with us."

At that point I had no idea what it was, but I knew that if it offered a chance to go in a new direction, I wouldn't hesitate. So the kids and I flew to Indiana. Little did I know that except for a brief trip back to sell everything I had, my time as a California girl was over.

My next trip to the Golden State would be five years later when I flew into San Francisco for the Gourmet Products Show, was interviewed on the radio, and saw our bakeware sold at Macy's Herald Square.

Family Business

[*Bette*]

Doughmakers was born on Christmas 1996. That was a memorable holiday season for a lot of reasons, not all of them the usual ones. My husband, Brooks, and I hosted all my brothers and sisters, plus their kids, at our house in Terre Haute. There was sharing. There was laughter. There was togetherness. But there was way too much vomiting.

Apparently there was more in the air that year than just the Christmas spirit. Of the thirty-six people staying in our house, twenty-one had the stomach flu. All four of the bathrooms were constantly occupied. And to think that just before the holidays I'd had new carpet installed. Talk about bad timing. I should have put down tarps instead.

In between "episodes" we grown-ups managed to talk shop. As Diane and Barb already knew, we'd called everyone together not just to renew family ties, but to discuss an idea for a business—one that we hoped to make a *family* business. The idea was endorsed quite strongly by Brooks, who had spent most of his career in the metals industry. At the time he had a company called Specialty Blanks, which produced pieces of metal that could be used by manufacturers to fabricate anything from satellite dishes to lighting fixtures. The story began when Brooks and our son Danny got involved in Cub Scouts. Frankly, I was trying very hard *not* to get involved. When you're a stay-at-home mom, you become a magnet for every volunteer organization under the sun. I didn't want to add "den mother" to my list of responsibilities, so I asked Brooks to take our son to the organizational meeting in hopes that if I wasn't there, I couldn't get drafted.

So my husband went to the gathering, and I didn't get drafted. Instead, he *volunteered* me.

I knew something was up when he walked in the door with a sheepish look on his face. Brooks said that during the meeting they kept asking for help but no one raised his hand, so *Brooks* did—for both of us. I became a den mother while he became Cubmaster of the whole pack.

As with most volunteer organizations, fund-raising was an endless problem. The Girl Scouts have it made in this department, selling their famous cookies. The Boy Scouts, as you may or may not know, sell popcorn. Well, it takes a lot of popcorn to keep a den, let alone a pack, solvent. We had around seventy-five boys in our Cub Scout pack, and at each month's meeting we'd spend $200 to $300 just to pay for the various merit badges they earned. Often the popcorn money couldn't cover the cost. The difference had to be made up with dues and other funds.

Unfortunately, that doesn't leave much money for special outings like the one Brooks had been planning for several months. It was a day trip, and not just across town: He wanted to take the Cubs to see the Cahokia Indian mounds near St. Louis, then to a Cardinals baseball game, and finally to see the Gateway Arch. And he wanted the parents and the brothers and sisters of the boys to be able to tag along if they chose. That meant we'd have to rent buses, and cover the cost of tickets and a bunch of other expenses—which meant we needed several thousand dollars.

That's an awful lot of popcorn.

But Brooks had an idea. Instead of selling the usual fund-raising item, what if the boys peddled simple, homemade cookie sheets? He would furnish the aluminum blanks, and the boys and their mothers—because that's always the way it is—would turn them into bakeware.

I wish I could say that I immediately grasped the world-shaking brilliance of this idea, but the truth is, I didn't see it.

That's the dumbest thing I've ever heard, I remember thinking.

But Brooks convinced us to give it a try. He had a bunch of aluminum blanks delivered to our garage, and then he brought in each den of Cub Scouts to work on them. We would clip and round the corners of each sheet using a hand-powered press and then stick each end into another wooden press that would bend the two ends into handles. *Voilà*, a cookie sheet. Once we got the hang of it, we produced them by the hundreds.

For starters we gave each boy twenty-five to sell. They were a huge hit. I think only three or four of the Cubs couldn't sell their entire allotment. One boy sold more than two hundred. Even better, the people who bought them said they were the best cookie sheets they'd ever used.

By the end of that first fund-raiser we had sold more than three thousand sheets at $4 a pop (two for $7, three for $10). Needless to say, we had enough cash to do St. Louis in style. Even better, we heard from more and more people about how impressed they were with the quality of the bakeware.

What made these cookie sheets so good? It had to do with how they were made and what they were made of. Aluminum is possibly the world's most oven-friendly metal. It heats much more evenly than steel, so if one part of the pan is at 350 degrees, you can bet that the rest is, too. Also, bright, shiny aluminum doesn't burn the bottoms of cookies or make thick, tough crusts on cakes and breads. Finally, our pans were made from specially textured sheeting that allowed air to flow under the baked goods. It was rare for anything to stick to them. Usually, cookies simply slide right off. And unlike coated products, our surface couldn't wear away because it was part of the sheet itself. Scratches didn't hurt a pan's performance because it was made of the same stuff all the way through. And aluminum, unlike steel, doesn't rust.

So why isn't all bakeware made of aluminum? Unfortunately, it's much more expensive than steel, and shaping it can be tricky. That's the reason the majority of what you see in stores today is made of steel that is encased in a nonstick coating. But nonstick coatings are usually very dark. This causes the pans to get very hot in the oven—similar to someone wearing a black suit on a summer day. You might think that would be a good thing, but a pan that gets too hot will scorch the bottoms of cookies. Also, steel doesn't heat all that evenly, producing erratic results. Cookies may be done perfectly on the left side of the pan but burn on the right.

I faced this problem many times myself. Brooks and I occasionally vacationed in furnished condos, where I sometimes found myself trying to make cookies or a cake using whatever bits of steel bakeware I rummaged from the kitchen cabinets. Not surprisingly, things would burn on the bottom before they were done on top. It was incredibly frustrating. Most people would blame themselves or their oven, but I knew it was the pan's fault.

The same uneven heating that ruins cookies and muffins will also cause the cheaper steel pans to twist and warp. Not that that's such a big problem for their makers: Steel bakeware's inherent weaknesses mean replacement pans have to be purchased regularly. When the nonstick coating gets scratched, the metal beneath it immediately begins to rust. Every few years even the occasional baker has to buy new pans.

Unless you purchased ours. Then you were pretty much set for life.

By the time we got through that first sale, I knew we were on to something. When Brooks and I were sharing our morning cup of coffee, the conversation would often drift to the pans. We even started tossing around possible names for them, such as Aunt Bette's Cookie Sheets. However, Brooks was busy with his business, and starting another company seemed to me like climbing Mount Everest.

Christmas was fast approaching, and a family reunion was just around the corner. Little did we know how excited my sisters would become about the concept—not to mention the actual bakeware. We must have used those cookie sheets nonstop in the days leading up to the holidays, baking everything from Sugar Cookie Cutouts (page 190) to an old recipe from Brooks's family, Swedish Red Lips (page 191). We probably baked about fifty dozen, all told. As usual our kitchen work resembled a Perry Como Christmas special. While we mixed dough, we'd sing either carols ("Silent Night" and "Silver Bells" were favorites) or songs our kids were memorizing for their school or church plays. We made mountains of cutout cookies but left them plain so we could have a cookie decorating party for all the young cousins.

These were tough conditions for the pans, but Barb and Diane were amazed at how well they worked. While I had visions of a cozy, small business selling to organizations for fund-raising, my sisters could sense a bigger opportunity. Perhaps it was all those wonderful aromas floating through the house, but they could smell the real potential. A small, family-owned business? Perhaps, to begin with. But who doesn't dream of making it big someday?

One night as we all sat on my porch having coffee late into the evening, the conversation turned quite serious. "What if" had come and gone. Now we were down to some serious business planning, and I was getting excited to see all that energy coming from my sisters.

In planning for the holidays I had particularly wanted to talk to Diane. She'd been going through some tough times, emotionally and financially. I wanted to get her into something with a future. Might this be it? I didn't know. For that matter, I didn't know if she'd be interested in doing something so completely different from anything she'd done before. But I wanted to try.

As she has already mentioned, we followed very different paths after leaving our parents' home. I became a hairdresser after graduating from high school in 1971 and landed a position at a salon in a huge New York nursing home. I did maybe forty wash and sets a day. My fingers turned blue from all the rinse jobs, but I earned $700 in a good week and more than $30,000 yearly. That was big money back then. To put it in perspective, it was almost twice what my father made after years on the job.

I met my husband-to-be, Brooks, in 1975, right after Christmas. My sister Bev and I and several of our girlfriends had gone skiing upstate. On the way back home we stopped to eat at a pub, and while we were sitting there, a guy with real short hair asked me to dance. I guessed he was in the service, so I figured it was my patriotic duty. Well, it turned out to be Brooks's college roommate. After a couple of turns around the dance floor, Brooks himself cut in. He was a six-foot-five Navy man. We danced and tried to talk, but the music was incredibly loud. He understood that my name was Bette, but somehow I got the idea that his was Duke.

"Duke" was stationed in Sarasota Springs, New York, where he worked in the Navy's nuclear power program. He memorized my phone number that evening and called me about a week later. When I picked up the phone, he said, "This is Brooks." But since I was under the impression that I didn't know anybody by that name—I knew a Duke but not a Brooks—I asked "Who?"

He refreshed my memory. After I finally got his name straight, we went out again, and again, and within three months we were engaged. Why the strong attraction? Maybe it was fate, although there could have been another reason. When I was a kid, every year at the beginning of school I would insist on getting a new sailor dress. I thought they were simply the neatest things in the world. My family ribbed me that my marrying a sailor was just a logical extension of my love of all things Navy-like.

After that, the changes came fast and furious. Brooks finished his service in the Navy, found a position at a place called Ontario Metal Supply, and, among other things, was put in charge of purchasing metal for the plant. Then in

1984, Brooks was recruited by Atlantic Richfield to join the aluminum rolling mill in Terre Haute, Indiana—a town on the western edge of the state with a population of around fifty-five thousand.

I'll never forget my first drive to Terre Haute from the Indianapolis airport as we visited Indiana to do some house hunting. I was thirty years old and had lived in Rochester, New York, my entire life. Now I was moving to the heartland and away from the family roots I relied on so much. The miles and miles of cornfields and soybeans seemed to underscore the coming separation. But I was happy for Brooks. He was making one of those "career moves" that men are always searching for.

Well, so much for a career. Ten months after moving to Indiana, Atlantic Richfield decided to divest itself of its metals companies. The Terre Haute plant, along with most of ARCO's aluminum assets, was sold to Alcan, and in the fall of 1987, Alcan drastically downsized the Terre Haute mill. Brooks could have stayed with the company, if he agreed to move to Cleveland. Instead, he and two of his fellow Alcan managers left to start their own company, Specialty Blanks. Like most new businesses, their first few years were lean and quite demanding. Then the company became profitable, and suddenly we had more money than we'd ever earned in our lives. When the partners sold the company in October 1997, we had enough cash to retire if we wanted to. But we didn't want to.

Which brings me back to the Christmas reunion of 1996. As I said before, one night during that now-legendary family gathering, we were sitting on our home's enclosed porch discussing the cookie sheet idea. Actually, fund-raising came up first. We all had kids, and at one time or another we had all found ourselves peddling doodads to our neighbors, trying to drum up money for schools or clubs or athletic organizations. Diane, Barb, and I talked about how ridiculous the process was and about the poor quality of many of the fund-raising items. Then we talked about how much everyone loved the cookie sheets. We decided that our best business model, at least to start, would be to market them as a fund-raising program to groups all over the country. Organizations could buy them for $5 each, mark up the price, and still give their customers a bargain—especially considering that the pans could last for decades.

It all seemed to make sense, and so, that very evening, the company was born. We even thought of the name. We decided we needed something that somehow mixed our three key ingredients: baking, the cookie sheet concept, and the idea of fund-raising. The name Doughmakers came up almost immediately.

Brooks listened quietly to our blue-sky dreaming. I think he was gathering data. He's so analytical that I call him Mr. Spreadsheet. Anyway, after taking in our ideas, he immediately started putting together the beginnings of a business plan, right there on the porch.

"Okay," he said after crunching a few numbers. "I think you should be able to sell $30,000 worth of pans this year."

That was probably my first taste of what we were really getting into. This wasn't amateur hour, this wasn't a fantasy, this was a real business that would require a tremendous amount of effort to build. I remember thinking, "There is no possible way we can sell that many cookie sheets."

But we were certainly going to try. Before we had gotten a business phone or printed stationery, Doughmakers was coming to life. My sister Barb immediately started surfing the Web for lists of conventions where we could sell our pans. And even better, Diane signed on wholeheartedly. I was elated but also more than a little scared.

We had a plan. We had a team. Now all we needed to do was build a manufacturing company from scratch.

The Real World

[Bette]

Looking around today at the Doughmakers headquarters, it's amazing to think how far we've come. Since 2000 we've resided in a custom-built, 50,000-square-foot manufacturing facility and command center. Of course it's the last word in industrial efficiency (Brooks, who oversaw design and construction, made sure of that), but it also reflects the unique nature of the company. One of our biggest selling points is that Doughmakers is, at heart, a woman's business. We wanted to showcase that difference by bringing in clubs and other groups for tours. That meant we couldn't make do with just another generic-looking, cubicle-packed corporate box.

Brooks emphasized that fact by adding an unorthodox architectural feature. Besides offices and loading docks, the Doughmakers headquarters also has a covered, columned wraparound porch that spans the entire front of the building. It makes it really easy for visitors to find us. All they have to do is look for the factory that doesn't look like a factory.

One of the building's most popular spots is the test kitchen. This is where Diane and I and a small group of much-appreciated volunteers labored to perfect the recipes included in this book. Some are winners from the 2003 Dough-makers Baking Contest; others were submitted by friends and family; and still others are concoctions that our grandmothers baked many years ago. This was back in the day when a recipe might call for a lump of butter "the size of an egg" or list all the ingredients but no amounts or offer proper measurements but make no mention of how everything should be combined. It was up to us to bring them into the twenty-first century by adding such "newfangled" touches as measured ingredients and baking instructions.

We spent about two weeks preparing dozens of dishes, from our Aunt Jessie's Orange Sunshine Cake (page 164) to the Fresh Blueberry Banana Bread (page 108). Talk about a fringe benefit for our staff: The entire building smelled like a bakery. People were answering phones with their mouths full and getting sticky icing on the handsets. Almost every day there were at least ten dishes sitting out on the counter in the employee cafeteria. We were actually begging people to take home the leftovers. We wondered if anybody would be able to work after stuffing themselves with sweets. I mean, is it really a good idea to gobble a couple of Chocolate Brownie Bars (page 82) chased with a slice of Carrot Pineapple Cake (page 149) and then try to accomplish something?

But there was one item that no one could be blasé about: Grandma Minnie's Date Nut Cake (page 156). When I was a child, it was a huge family favorite—and definitely *my* number one choice. It's incredibly moist and is coated with a thick, wonderful cream cheese icing. Well, the day I made it, everybody who tasted it was beside themselves. There were certainly no leftovers on that occasion.

Putting together all those recipes was hard but gratifying. Fortunately, we're used to such labor. Almost from day one, hard work and long hours have been part and parcel of the business. Our company started out as a dream, but it took tremendous effort to get us to the point where we have a custom-built headquarters, a test kitchen, and dozens of hungry, sweets-craving employees.

Our beginnings were considerably more modest. The first "plant" was Brooks's and my two-car garage, followed by a 400-square-foot rented room in a factory. I spent much of my time making pans, processing orders, and looking after the "big picture." The only thing was, at that time the picture wasn't all that big.

As soon as Diane wrapped things up in California, she returned to Terre Haute and pitched in. I wish I could describe in words how hard she worked— and not just at Doughmakers. This was a start-up company, so we didn't have a pile of money. Brooks and I provided the early financing, but it wasn't enough to give us paychecks. I didn't get paid for a year and a half, and Diane didn't see a dime for a year. To make ends meet she worked at the local Red Lobster and at the Chinese restaurant owned by our sister-in-law, Pauline (Rich's wife). When she finished there at around 10 P.M., she'd report to Doughmakers and make pans until around 2 or 3 A.M. It was exhausting, but as Diane said, she'd worked just as hard on jobs where she had no stake in the company and no prospects of benefiting from success. This time she was working on something that might actually pay off.

But there was still a mountain of labor between us and success. We both made hundreds of pans, usually working different schedules. I clipped and bent during the daylight hours, while Diane pulled the night shift. Working this way, we produced three hundred to four hundred pans daily.

Finally, with some inventory on the shelf, we started to travel and sell at shows around the country. Over the next few months a steady stream of positive feedback poured in from people who had bought our cookie sheets and tried them in their kitchens. We received calls, emails, and letters from people everywhere telling us how much they liked our product. They were so impressed with our sheets that we decided to file for a patent as well as a trademark on our name for the metal's texture, The *Original Pebble Pattern*® surface. Still, we made our pans one at a time, by hand, with personal, painstaking attention.

And then things got complicated. In October 1997 we hired our first employee, Joyce McClelland, a friend of mine whom I'd known since moving to Indiana (and the proud author of the Homemade Hamburger Buns recipe on page 120, and the Texas Sheet Cake on page 154). At the time we were still headquartered in our home, but things were getting a bit cramped. Then in 1998, not too long after we'd organized as a corporation, we moved to a small, 1,300-square-foot building. But our fax line and business phone were still at our house. Diane and I were so busy making pans and promoting them that there was nobody around during business hours to take calls. When I got home at night, I was overwhelmed with messages. As I sifted through them, I couldn't help wondering how many others we'd missed. Joyce had been helping us sell pans, so we brought her in full-time as a secretary. She watched the phones and helped with the books and did a great job, though she did have trouble keeping her clothes on.

Let me explain. Our oldest daughter had just gone off to college, so we turned her upstairs bedroom into an office. The only problem was that the room got hot enough to bake bread, and Joyce is very warm-blooded. But she

Bette (top), *in the office/plant on Margaret Avenue in Terre Haute, with Joyce* (left) *and Debbie, who shared a desk where their knees were touching through most of the day. They have a little more room now.*

found a way to stay comfortable. Since most of the time Diane and I were either making cookie sheets or on the road, she was usually on her own in the house. If things got too muggy upstairs, she'd just take off her blouse. And if she heard someone come in the front door, she'd quickly put it back on. For obvious reasons she tried to keep her temperature control system a secret, but we eventually found out. She was and remains extremely embarrassed about it. I'm sure she wouldn't want the entire world to know, but it's just too funny not to share. Joyce contributed a great story to Doughmakers lore, and I'm afraid we just gave it to the world.

One of Joyce's other contributions was to remind us that we needed to pay careful attention to our workmanship. As an avid baker she knew what kind of bakeware was available in the stores. She, too, could see the potential for Doughmakers, and the quality of the pans was not to be ignored. Joyce was always reminding us to watch for sharp edges and inspect for defects. When Joyce would tell us this, we thought, "Oh, crud. Now we have something else to think about." And a lot more work to do. Fixing the sharp edges meant adding a complicated, drawn-out step to our manufacturing process. Originally we could turn an aluminum blank into a finished pan in a couple of minutes, but now we had to file the edges. As we soon discovered, this simple-sounding task took a considerable amount of skill and time to do properly. If you filed the edges too hard or incorrectly, you could actually make them sharper.

We experimented with all sorts of filing systems, trying to find one that was both effective and efficient. In the end the one that worked best was, of course, the most labor-intensive. Good old hand files got the best results. This is one of the reasons that in the early days Diane and I made most of our inventory. Filing was a tricky process that took forever for new hires to accomplish. Plus it was such awful work that almost no one wanted to do it. Until we finally got machinery to do it, only Diane and I, plus a few trusted friends and family members, were cleared to create Doughmakers products.

The constant push to make more cookie sheets was incredibly grueling. As sales ramped up, we pushed ourselves to the point of exhaustion. Local sales of Advil spiked as we constantly tended to sore muscles. Eventually we both had surgery to correct carpal tunnel syndrome. There were also constant cuts and scrapes, plus the fact that the filing literally wore off all our fingerprints. But nothing could stop us. We made pans by the thousands. We would bring in a pallet of metal containing a thousand blanks and then go through it in about two days.

I guess that's one of the reasons that Diane and I got so tired of hearing some people gush about how wonderful it must be to have our own business. They thought we set our own hours, made a lot of money, and answered to no one. But unless they owned a small business themselves, they didn't understand that before any of those good things could happen, the small entrepreneur must work every waking hour, do everything her- or himself, and live on virtually no money for far longer than is comfortable. The ones who did own their own businesses were always very supportive and encouraging. I don't think they'd envy the way we begged for bank loans, signed over our homes, and then made a personal guarantee on top of that. Yet that's what we did. Most people wouldn't risk everything for a dream. Maybe we're just more optimistic. Or maybe we're off our rockers.

The pan-filing crisis was just one of a never-ending series of big and small challenges. Even the littlest things would fray my nerves. I remember obsessing about getting boxes in which to ship the pans. I think that at the time they cost about $1 apiece. I fretted about how that would affect our bottom line. Also, how many cookie sheets could we ship at one time? Originally we crammed forty-two into each box, but we had to cut that down because the gross weight was close to 50 pounds. Many of our clients were older women, and sometimes they would call to tell us that UPS had deposited a box on their front porch that was so heavy they couldn't move it. So we cut the number to a more manageable twenty per box.

We got a taste of shipping problems early on. We were still in our first years as a company when UPS went on strike. We used to simply pile up a mountain of boxes and let the regular delivery guy take them away, but during the strike we had to lug every one of them to the post office ourselves. We would fill up the back of my Chrysler minivan with about twenty of them. I had Terre Haute's only low-rider minivan.

The weight issue was constantly popping up. Especially on those rare occasions when Diane would fly to shows rather than drive. One time she simply couldn't bring herself to pay to have cookie sheets shipped out, so she decided to hide two cases' worth—about 100 pounds—in her luggage. Joyce went to this show, too, and she was packing exactly the same weight. When Diane, puffing and sweating, finally dragged her bags to the check-in counter and tried to drop them off, she found out that one of them alone weighed 70 pounds. The attendant took one look at that and told her she needed to charge her for an extra piece of luggage.

But Diane was adamant. "I can't afford it," she told the lady.

So they went back and forth for a couple of minutes. The attendant said she shouldn't worry because her company would pay for it. Diane said she *was* the company and that's exactly why she couldn't afford to pay. Finally they let her through, overstuffed suitcases and all. But after that, whenever Diane took a plane to a show, she made sure nobody else picked up her luggage.

Browbeating airline personnel was just one of the many talents that blossomed in Diane after she signed on with Doughmakers. She turned out to be good at sales, good at logistics, and good at making the darn pans. I can honestly say that without her involvement, I don't know how we'd have survived those first years. It's hard to believe that when she first came to Terre Haute, I wondered if she would have much of a role beyond manufacturing. Frankly, I didn't see her as a strong communicator. She just wasn't (or so I thought) the kind of person who could go out, meet the public, and tell the Doughmakers story. For that matter I had plenty of doubts about my own talents in that department.

But she can really sell. In fact, she was much, much better at shows than I could ever be, mainly because I hated to travel. So early on, Diane said that if I liked doing other things, she'd do the majority of the road work. I couldn't have been happier, though my days of cross-country driving are still not entirely over. Currently I mostly attend retail trade gatherings where I bake cookies and talk to buyers for chains and independent kitchen stores. I've made several trips to QVC for on-air sales (once at 4 A.M.), and I teach cooking classes in our retail stores. The relatively small number of direct-selling shows that I do now are mostly to keep my hand in and to help resolve last-minute scheduling problems. For instance, years ago I worked the Cleveland Home and Garden Show solo for ten days. Diane was supposed to relieve me, but she was deathly ill, so I stayed on alone from 10 A.M. to 9 P.M., talking nonstop.

That's par for the course, but what made it really tough was that I was parked next to one of those places that sells hand-powered vegetable choppers. All day long the guys were demonstrating the darn things and doing their spiel over loudspeakers. I'd have tears in my eyes from their onions! But at the end of the show they paid me a great compliment, saying they liked the energetic way I worked my booth. Coming from the hand-powered vegetable chopper guys, that's high praise indeed.

Diane and I have thousands of stories like that from the early days. Sure it was tough, but all those tribulations helped us learn about our company from the bottom up. That knowledge would come in handy as Doughmakers evolved from basically a two-woman operation into a company with more than forty employees.

On the Road Again and Again and Again

[Diane]

I always get a kick out of Ruth Clark, our almost superhumanly friendly Doughmakers receptionist. She's a very hard worker and possibly the perkiest person on God's green earth. Ask her how she's doing, and she'll invariably say, "Wonderful!" I'm pretty sure she'd say that even if she'd just had to change a flat tire in a driving rain on her way to work.

Not that the woman doesn't enjoy her free time. In fact, she makes a hobby out of anticipating the weekend. When I was on the road on business, I'd call the office, and she'd always have some calendar-related comment. It's hump day. It's Thursday. It's this. It's that. And I'd get a little wistful, thinking, "Wouldn't it be great if Friday was exciting?"

For six years I worked pretty much every Saturday and Sunday. The weekend only meant that I had another Doughmakers show to do. This was just one of the ways my life was utterly transformed by that Christmas gathering at Bette's house. In spite of the flu situation, the reunion was a blast. And I was very excited about joining the new business because, in truth, I was desperate. Trapped in go-nowhere jobs and worried about my kids' futures, I was looking for any sort of safety net. Under those circumstances, moving to the Midwest and into the bosom of my family sounded irresistibly warm and fuzzy. It was a godsend.

But remember the old saying, "Heaven helps those who help themselves"? That was certainly true for me. I'd been given a chance for a new life, but I would have to earn it. From the moment I signed on with Doughmakers, I was in it up to my neck. After the Christmas gathering broke up, I left my kids in Terre Haute with Bette, flew home, held the mother of all garage sales, and then hopped on a plane back to the Midwest.

Once I got back, Bette and I immediately started making pans, loading her minivan, and hitting the highway. I was the road warrior, going wherever, whenever, to sell our goods and promote our company. Bette traveled a lot, too, but she also had to run the manufacturing side, process orders, and occasionally check the map to make sure we were headed in the right direction.

A few words about the shows we did in those days. Organizations ranging from PTAs to Lions to Key Clubs to cheerleaders to soccer teams to women's clubs all have national and regional conventions. Most of these include exhibition areas where, among other things, visitors can look at products that might make good fund-raising items. This initially was Doughmakers' niche. We wanted to offer these folks our pans in the hope that they'd order hundreds or even thousands for their members to sell. This proved an amazingly lucrative market, not just because organizations would order, say, a gross of cookie sheets but because the thousands of people attending these events would also buy individual Doughmakers products to take home.

Now you know why we did (and continue to do) somewhere between sixty and seventy-five shows and fairs each year. These can last anywhere from a single day to more than two weeks. In the early days I would do about forty-five of them, often solo. Think about that for a minute: forty-five a year, almost all of them on weekends. Since there are only fifty-two weeks in a year, you can bet that at almost any given time I was either packing to go to a show, working a show, or unpacking after a show.

Ruth Clark.

Sherri and Diane Perdieu (left) *at a General Federation of Women's Clubs convention promoting Doughmakers fund raising.*

Our sales program, just like everything else, started out small. It had to, because our entire stock of pans consisted of whatever Bette and I managed to make. Sometimes we would work all night and then leave the next day for a show. That first year we put about sixty-three thousand miles on Bette's minivan.

During the early days Bette and I sometimes traveled together. One of our very first shows was just up the road in Indianapolis. We were so inexperienced, we didn't even take a dolly to haul around our bakeware. That was a serious mistake, because a box full of baking sheets is heavy—especially when you try to hustle it through a crowded convention center while wearing heels.

We came away from those very early shows totally jazzed, thinking we were the greatest salespeople of all time. *Everybody* wanted our product. I can remember talking to Bette after one show about a particularly enthusiastic "customer."

"One lady wanted to take twelve sheets," I said excitedly.

Of course, it's easy to sell when you're giving it away, literally. We had reasoned that if we handed out free samples to the people who attended fund-raising shows, they'd try them out, like them, and place orders—which tells you how incredibly green we were. It took a few shows before we realized that no one took us seriously *because* we gave our stuff away. So we started charging $5 a sheet. That changed everything. When we placed a value on our product, other people did, too. The shows became gold mines—and not for the reasons we'd originally envisioned. We booked a decent number of orders from fund-raising groups, but we also sold thousands of dollars' worth of pans, cash and carry, to attendees. In fact, we were a bona fide phenomenon. While the typical vendor might be happy to clear, say, $1,000 a day at a show, we did that much routinely. After a few years, and with a few more types of pans to offer, we could sell $10,000 in merchandise on particularly good days.

As the years went by, the cash flow from selling direct to consumers was too appealing to ignore, and fund-raising-focused shows began to fall away. Summer was filled with state and county fairs, but the holiday shopping season (September through early December) was our busiest time. We hit every apple festival and Christmas show we could find. And as Doughmakers grew, so did our booth—and the hassles involved in getting it ready. In the beginning, setup was a breeze. All we had was a 10-by-10 rented space. We put up a folding table, covered it with a vinyl tablecloth, hung a hand-lettered sign, and set out our cookie sheets. No problem.

But things didn't stay simple for long. We realized that cookie cutters could attract customers to our booth, where we could sell them on the pans. So we added a few, and then a few more. At one point we offered some three hundred different items besides the pans we made. Setting them out was like stocking an entire store every weekend. They were popular, and that's pretty much the only kind thing I can say about them. I can't tell you how many times we loaded and unloaded crates of cookie cutters. We had so many gimcracks sitting around the plant, they were literally falling off the shelves. That really burned my biscuits.

Hustling all this onto trucks was a huge operation. In the beginning we got along with Bette's long-suffering minivan, but soon we were packing our "metal" (Doughmakers slang for bakeware) into a 25-foot box truck, sometimes with a 20-foot trailer attached. It took two days to fill all the bins, and then maybe another half day to get all those thousands of pounds of metal on the truck. Some shows were so big we needed a second truck.

Most of these events took at least a day to reach. Once there, we'd have another day or maybe even a day and a half to set up the booth. We tried to organize things so that they came off the truck in some sort of logical order, but this was more art than science. New employees on their first (and even second and third) shows would inevitably get totally lost. Of course the fault was partly mine. There was simply no way for me to adequately explain how to set up a booth. Newbies could only watch and learn.

Sometimes we'd have as many as four or five staffers along for larger, longer events. Most shows ran from 9 A.M. to 9 P.M., so everyone was usually trapped in a windowless building for most of every day and evening. We'd work until closing, spend an hour restocking, get something to eat, then count money until, perhaps, 1 A.M. Then it was off to bed . . . and back to work at 6 or 7 the next morning. On particularly long trips, sleep deprivation could be just as big a problem as tight muscles and sore feet.

Fortunately, departures were always much easier than arrivals, mainly because there was a lot less stuff to put in the truck. Nine times out of ten we would leave immediately, put in a few hours on the road, and then get a hotel room for the night. The next morning we'd light out for Terre Haute. Once home we spent a day unloading. We put everything back in its proper place, right down to the last whisk and pie pan. Then, a few days later, we did it all over again.

My solo trips could sometimes get particularly "interesting," because if something unexpected happened, there was no one to back me up. I couldn't even take a bathroom break without abandoning the booth in the middle of a show. My usual strategy was to wait until a particularly sweet-looking woman came along. Then I'd ask her to just sort of linger for a few moments while I ran to the ladies' room. I only wanted them to stand there, but often as not, I'd come back to find them selling pans left and right. They were adorable. Things like that gave me a renewed faith in humanity—that and the fact that for years we didn't get a single rubber check from our customers. We even had people who, if they accidentally got one too many pans at a show, would mail the extra back to us. I guess bakers are just more considerate than your average citizen.

At the beginning of each new event we were usually excited, because we wanted to beat last year's sales figures. Toward the middle of the trip the excitement faded, to say the least; we were sick and tired and hot and homesick. But then, as the end approached, we suddenly didn't want it to be over. Why the change of heart? Because we had spent a week or more bonding with the

Joyce McClelland, Doughmakers' first employee, restocking for the Kansas City Home Show. Joyce now answers our customer service line, glad to be (mostly) retired from the road.

folks in the other booths. I can remember the first time I did the Minnesota State Fair, which deserves a spot in the Doughmakers Hall of Fame as one of the toughest and most demanding of all the big events. It runs for almost two weeks during the dog days of August and the first few days of September.

The good part is that we sell a lot of product there. The bad part is that we were stuck in a giant building with no air-conditioning. The temperature was generally 10 degrees warmer than whatever it was outside—and it never seemed to dip below 90 degrees outside. There was a giant, antique-looking fan way up in the rafters, but all it did was stir up this strange black dust that gave everyone severe coughs. So we were constantly taking the dolly out to the truck to get more product, hacking and coughing through the dusty air. But for some reason we didn't want it to end. We had made friends and, let's be truthful, we had also made a lot of cash. Every day at Minnesota we did around $6,000 to $8,000 in sales. When you are surrounded by buddies and making money as fast as you can collect it, who can ask for more?

Still, even though the people were nice, the work was almost always tough. At some show sites we had to park the truck half a mile from the building. When it was time to stock or restock the booth, someone had to drag a dolly out to the truck, load up, and then drag it back over the asphalt, up a ramp to the building, and across a crowded exhibition hall to our booth. Not surprisingly, we tried to bring in as much as possible on each run. Usually we packed the dolly chin-high with about 300 pounds of product, all held in place with bungee cords. At major events we might perform this ritual four times a day in rain, snow, bitter cold, or boiling heat (because, as anyone who has done this kind of work knows, it's always either raining, snowing, bitterly cold, or boiling hot during shows).

Sometimes it seemed as if the venue itself conspired to increase our misery. I remember one building in Tulsa with a dolly ramp that was as steep as the first hill on a roller coaster. I watched three people almost get killed trying to push their gear up that ramp. I had to jump in front of one lady's hand cart to keep her from being crushed. I mean, does it take a rocket scientist to design an entrance ramp that can actually be used as such?

Maybe it does, because almost no one could get this little detail right. In Arizona I piled about 400 pounds of hardware onto a dolly. It was so hot, people were actually passing out on the sidewalks. I almost had a stroke just getting to the building. Finally, I made it to the entrance, only to find another one of those super-steep ramps. I had so much weight on the dolly that I was doubled over pushing it. Well, there were three able-bodied men at the top of the ramp, watching me and laughing. They were actually betting on whether I'd make it. I saw all this out of the corner of my eye, and you can't imagine how mad I was. I mean, they didn't even ask if they could help. No, they were going to see if I fell down and got run over. And then what? Somebody would win five bucks? On days like that I wished we'd never come up with aluminum bakeware. Why not something light, like a feather duster?

One of my most heartbreaking mishaps also took place at the infamous Minnesota State Fair. I was hauling a cart full of cookie cutters. I tried to do it one-handed, because I was also carrying an even more vital piece of equipment: a triple latte. Caffeine was my lifeblood during long, grueling shows. That day something went wrong. The cart went flying, my latte went flying, and the cookie cutters went *everywhere*. But as I stood there looking at the carnage, all I could think was, "I paid three bucks for that latte." I wanted to sit down on the curb and cry.

Actually, my scariest moments on the road weren't the times I was almost crushed under mountains of metal. The true moments of uneasiness came when I was walking around carrying gigantic, horse-choking wads of money. People at shows paid with cash and checks, but because we were so busy during the day, I couldn't dash off and deposit it at a bank. So the greenbacks just piled up and up and up. (Thankfully, we have a better, much safer system now.)

Yet in spite of all the cash we used to carry, we were robbed only once—And I'm guessing the heist didn't work out nearly as well as the robber expected. It happened to Bette at the Minnesota State Fair (why was it always the Minnesota State Fair?). She had to cover for me one year when I was knocked out by the flu. After a particularly long day, she and the crew decided to get something to eat at a barbecue stand on the grounds. Bette was carrying her purse and two bags: a plastic one containing about $15,000 in cash and a cloth one from our bank containing a coworker's dress shoes. Bette got her food and sat down on a bench near a line of trees. She had just started eating when she suddenly got the overwhelming feeling that someone was behind her. She spun around just in time to see a guy crawling up behind the bench and reaching for one of the bags.

Bette jumped up and started screaming. The guy grabbed the bank bag, leaped to his feet, and ran off. Bette took a few quick steps and immediately twisted her ankle. She tried to run to the barbecue stand, all the while shouting, "Help, he's got my money! He's got my money!" Instantly the cook and several of the men in line took off after the crook. They chased him, we later learned, for almost twenty minutes. He got away only after he climbed over a barbed-wire-topped fence, slicing himself up pretty thoroughly in the process.

But here's the rub: As the chase went on, Bette limped back to the bench to reclaim her purse and the remaining bag, but now she remembered that the bank bag didn't hold the money. It was in the plastic bag, which was still sitting there safe and sound. The crook had endured quite a bit of pain and suffering just to swipe a pair of pumps.

"I would have loved to see his face when he opened that bag and saw those shoes," Bette told me. I bet they weren't even his color.

As Bette said, this was an awful lot of trouble to go to for bakeware—especially when not every show was a winner or even an also-ran. Once we drove all the way to Colorado for a one-day event, set up our booth, and didn't sell a single thing. But my biggest disappointment had to be the Soroptimist convention we attended in New York City. We had such high hopes that we actually paid an exorbitant fee to ship in additional metal. I also took Mom along, and we stayed (thanks to Brooks' travel points) on the fortieth floor of the Marriott Marquis at Times Square. Our idea was to work the event, make a bunch of money, and then maybe eat someplace nice and go to a Broadway musical—a working vacation.

It didn't happen that way. The show was way too "international" for Doughmakers. About 75 percent of the attendees were Japanese women who, though very wealthy, couldn't speak or read a word of English. So there I sat, unable to communicate, trying to sell these women baking sheets that were probably bigger than their whole oven. The first day I sold two pans; the second day, none.

We were bleeding money—it cost $40 a day just to park our van—and our spirits were even lower than our sales total. Finally, in complete desperation, I accosted one of the Japanese interpreters and asked her to make a special sign for me. We had just introduced pizza pans into our lineup, so I had her write, in Japanese characters, "Sushi Serving Tray." Then I got some carryout sushi, arranged it on a pizza pan, and put up the sign. I swear, the very next person to walk by bought six. While I'm taking the lady's money, my mom is sitting on the stool behind me, saying in a low voice that only I could hear, "My daughter is brilliant . . ."

I was about ready to believe it myself, but that was our last sale for the entire show. Needless to say, it was a very long drive home.

Although we had some high-profile bombs, we also enjoyed some unexpected successes. Toward the end of my time on the road, we did a tiny show in Milwaukee that was sponsored by *Taste of Home* magazine. By then we were doing huge events—ten days long, with thousands of vendors—so this gathering, which contained maybe thirty booths, seemed like a disaster waiting to happen. That is, until the show started. Most of the other exhibitors turned out to be information booths with some free samples. Almost no one else had something to sell, so anyone with a few bucks in his or her pocket gravitated toward us. At all times we had a 20-foot-long line of women in front of our booth, standing there ever so patiently, waiting to buy. All we did was hand out pans, take money, and deposit it in the cash register. We easily did $2,000 in sales per hour. It was sweet. We were in show heaven. Three days like that could make up for ten thousand miles of driving.

Selling 101

[*Diane*]

On the road there was no escape from work. Not even when I slept. Sometimes, when I got into a town too late to set up the booth the night before a show, I had to do it early the next morning before the doors opened. But I might as well have sat up and worked, for all the rest I got. Every time I closed my eyes and drifted off, I was at the show site, hauling things out of bins. By the time the sun rose, I'd rearranged the booth dozens of times in my dreams. So I guess you could say that when it came to selling, I'd eat, breathe, and sleep Doughmakers.

I obsessed so much because laying out the booth properly could mean the difference between a lousy show and a great one. In sales, as I slowly came to realize, the devil is in the details. It's in how you merchandise your booth. It's in what you say to customers and even in whether or not you make eye contact with a client. Over the years I developed a set of rules for turning those potential customers into buyers. I didn't learn these rules in business school but in the school of hard knocks.

Considering where I've been in my life, the idea of my dispensing "sales tips" is almost funny. If you had met me in the pre-Doughmakers era, you would never have imagined that one day I would be responsible for moving millions of dollars of merchandise or that in a single day I could convince hundreds of strangers to buy my product. And I wouldn't have believed it, either.

Looking back, I realize that I must always have possessed some innate selling ability. Bette thinks we picked up the basics of salesmanship while working as hairdressers. I'm inclined to agree. Hairdressers have excellent people skills. The really successful ones can engage their clients in seemingly frivolous conversations and then sift through their words to figure out exactly what they want. And once you find out what a person really wants, you can provide it.

Well, I could certainly do that. But before I could apply my hairdressing skills to bakeware, I had to revolutionize my attitude and approach. As Bette said, when I first joined Doughmakers, she wasn't sure what to do with me. We all figured I'd start out in manufacturing. Using me as a salesperson didn't seem like a very good fit. After all, I didn't have sales experience or even, it seemed on the surface, much in the way of people skills. So Bette had to teach me some.

These sometimes useful, sometimes embarrassing, sometimes infuriating informal training sessions came to be called—by the two of us, at least—refinement classes. Bette believed I was much too rough around the edges to deal with the public, so she endeavored to help me fit in with polite company by showing me appropriate business attire, getting me to cut back on the swearing, on and on and on.

Yes, I know this sounds incredibly overbearing and presumptuous—and there were times when I would have heartily agreed with that view—but I have to admit that when I first joined the company, I was like a cookie that had been baked on a steel pan: I was tough, and I'd been burned. In retrospect, Bette's advice was incredibly helpful and probably essential to my later success. But there were times when my opinions about "refinement classes" were a lot less charitable. A button I bought for Bette summed it up. It read, "Save yourself some time. Just assume I know everything." Oh, was she offended when I handed it to her. That was fine, because at the time I was highly offended by *her*. It wasn't a constant thing, but arguments flared between us. I think a certain level of bickering was inevitable, considering the stress and fatigue we faced, along with the fact that we were together so much.

It's been quite a while since anything remotely argumentative has happened between us. We don't yell at each other anymore. And even more important, I don't yell at anyone *else* anymore. That's quite an attitude adjustment for someone who was once infamous for saying what was on her mind, often loudly and at great length, and not particularly caring who heard.

I'm happy to say that when it comes to my emotions, I can now express myself in more low-key ways.

But if I had to change my outlook in order to market Doughmakers, Bette had to change hers in order to get along with me. We went back and forth over this for the better part of three years. I think we began to accept each other for who we were rather than who we wished we were. Bette, for lack of a better phrase, relinquished her powers over me. Instead of a remodeling project, I became her friend and sister. That new understanding (as well as the refinement classes) gave me a huge boost while we were feeling our way forward, trying to figure out a recipe for successful selling.

Based on our experiences, I developed a system for engaging people's interest, chatting them up, finding out which of our products' various "sell points" pushed their buttons, and then catering to that interest to make a sale. All this had to happen very quickly because show attendees have the attention span of gnats. I figured I had about thirty seconds with each potential customer who drifted by the booth. So, first thing, I made eye contact and held it. If you don't have that, chances are you won't make the sale. The whole time you're talking about the pans, they'll be glancing around at other booths.

Once I had that all-important eye contact, this, more or less, is what I'd say: "Have you heard about Doughmakers bakeware before? Can I tell you what makes our product better? First of all, it's made out of solid aluminum, very heavy gauge. That means they won't rust. The pebble design you see is pressed right into the metal, and it creates an easy-release surface without a coating or worries about scratching. They're shiny because that gives you even browning in the oven. Dark nonstick coatings can cause burning on the bottom of your cookies because the dark color draws heat in the oven. Also, since ours are extra-thick, you don't get any buckling or warping. And they wash up beautifully. Because of the pebble design, food releases easily. We're having a special today. If you buy one of the formed cake pans, you can pick a free cookie sheet or pizza pan."

Don't try this at home, but after years of practice I can say all that in one breath and not sound rushed.

Hopefully one of those selling points (It's shiny! It browns evenly! It won't rust! It won't warp!) would catch the customer's attention. I usually knew when this happened because people's eyes really do light up when they're interested in something. For example, I might mention that our pans don't rust, then look at them and see that they were thinking, *"Holy cow, all mine rust."* And then I knew what they wanted. Every salesman knows that people don't buy products, they buy solutions to their problems. Not clothes, but a way to look better and be more comfortable. Not shoes, but an end to aching feet. Not shiny bakeware, but the key to perfect cakes, pies, and cookies.

We gave people those solutions—not the hard sell. If you wanted that sort of thing, you could always walk down the aisle to where the guys in headset microphones were hawking cookware made from "surgical steel." *That's* hard-core selling. I never lied or exaggerated, and never got loud or aggressive. Some show vendors are old-fashioned snake oil salesmen, and many show attendees know it. We, on the other hand, never tried to be anything other than what we were: two moms with something good to sell. And I think that honesty shone through.

Early on we discovered we had one important ally: the pans' textured surface. It drew people like a light draws moths. Passersby saw the surface and walked over and rubbed their fingers lightly over the pattern. Well, the minute someone's index finger hit that surface, they got to hear all about it. If the person's eyes rolled or drifted while I spoke, I would usually wrap things up and release them. But if they listened attentively, I'd run through my entire presentation.

Our booth was our other big selling tool. As I said earlier, in the beginning they were small and sparse. That wasn't always a bad thing—especially when it came time to pack up and leave. At the end of some of our first shows we walked past people who were breaking down massive spaces containing hundreds of items. I'd think, *"See ya, suckers,"* and head for the parking lot. A year or two later that was *me* turning out the lights as I left.

Over the years the booths grew in size to as big as 40 by 30 feet. We filled all that real estate with more and more pans, plus those hundreds of little doodads I used to enjoy hauling around so much.

Setting up the booth properly was vital because the smallest things could affect sales volume. For instance, you couldn't overestimate the importance of placement. If a particular item wasn't selling, sometimes all you had to do was move it to a different display area. Then it would sell like mad, though I have no idea why. Sales could also hinge on whether an item was positioned high or low. As anyone who has ever shopped in a grocery store knows, eye level is the sweet spot. And believe it or not, ground level is pretty good, too. But anything above eye level is death. People simply won't tilt their heads back. And this isn't just a trade show thing. Visit one of the giant retailers, such as Wal-Mart or Costco, and you'll see that while merchandise is displayed to a height of maybe six feet, any space higher than that is used for storage.

Some rules of booth design were a bit more logical. Most important, a booth had to have an obvious entrance and exit so that a rational traffic flow developed. I know this sounds pretty basic, but if you don't do it right and the booth becomes congested, then three or four people prowling around can look like fifty to passersby. Potential customers might glance over, decide we looked too busy, and keep walking. But if they saw some logic in the scheme and a way to get in and out, they'd come in.

Unfortunately, you can't perfect a booth's design until you've watched a fair number of people move through it—which is why anybody who worked with me knew they'd probably have to set up the booth twice: the first time when we arrived and the second time that night, to take advantage of lessons learned. If the flow wasn't right, rather than grind my teeth over the money we were losing, I'd rip up everything after closing time and start over. It wasn't pretty, but most of the time it had to be done.

When I wasn't rearranging our booth or giving the thirty-second Doughmakers spiel, I'd glance around at other people's goods. Time and again I'd see what to me were obvious selling blunders. For instance, I feel it's vitally important to market your product energetically. If someone looks interested, engage them in conversation. Don't wait for them to come to you because they won't. Yet I'd always see tiny mom-and-pop booths filled with beautiful crafts that probably pulled in only $300 in daily sales, if that. The reason was that the owners invariably built little "nests" in one corner, complete with a folding chair, TV, radio, and maybe even their dog. They'd sit there and eat, drink, read the paper, or snooze while the world went by—and the world did indeed go right by them.

While I'm sure building a nest is quite cozy, I never allowed it. The point of these shows wasn't to be comfortable. When you're smack in the middle of a six-hundred-booth exposition, that's a recipe for mediocrity. Food wasn't allowed in our area, and neither were chairs. Everyone stood at all times. It sounds as if we're slave drivers, but the truth is, if someone sees you sitting down, they instinctively don't want to bother you. They think you're resting. Eating is an even bigger turnoff because then people *really* think they're bugging you. But if you're standing and engaging them in conversation, they don't feel bad at all. Maybe they'll stay and talk. Maybe they'll buy a cookie sheet. So if you wanted to sit or eat, you had to go someplace else.

Having a thick skin was almost as big an asset as tough feet. Whenever I took employees to shows, I told them not to get discouraged if the first twenty people they approached didn't buy. The thing to remember was that there was a lot of money floating around those places, and if we worked hard, we'd get our share. Maybe only 10 percent of the thousands of people we talked to each day bought something, but that 10 percent would in turn talk to thousands of others. So for every pan we sold face-to-face, maybe we sold another by word of mouth.

These techniques worked, but they were hard. After twelve hours we sometimes wondered how we'd pry our shoes off our swollen feet and whether we could make it to the nearest eatery without fainting. And often, after talking for half a day, I didn't have any voice left. One time in the midst of a big show I called to talk to my son. I was so hoarse, he didn't believe it was me. He said, "This isn't Mommy. This is Uncle Rich. Quit playing with me."

No doubt about it, selling isn't for sissies.

The great thing about selling Doughmakers' products was that even when I was alone, I still had plenty of help. After a couple of years we started seeing the same faces at our booths—people who had purchased our products and were either back for more or back to share stories of how their baked goods had improved. They were our groupies, and we affectionately called them Doughheads. Often they'd hang around chatting for ten minutes or ask us if we'd added anything new to our line. They'd get so excited about how much the business had grown that they'd get us excited, too.

They were the best all-volunteer sales force in the world. Time and again when a potential customer was weighing whether to buy a pan, he or she would chime in with glowing testimonials. Let me tell you, nothing can convert a reluctant buyer quicker than having two or three people at the booth tell her, in no uncertain terms, "Buy the pans. These ladies are telling the truth. I bought them last year. They're my favorites, and I'm back for more." This happened all the time and continues to happen. Seeing and talking to our Doughheads is one of the things that makes this job fun.

Those encounters more than made up for the occasional odd ducks we dealt with. I remember one lady who seemed a few cookies shy of a baker's dozen. We used to sell really cool cookie cutters shaped like mittens. This woman asked if we had any left-handed models. I explained that you could make a perfectly serviceable left-handed mitten just by flipping the cutter over, but for some reason this information didn't process. "No, I need a left-handed mitten," she kept insisting.

Sometimes I wondered how folks like that made it to the show. Maybe someone dropped them off, because I sure couldn't imagine them driving. She wasn't the worst, however.

Most of the folks who bought our pans caught onto the "won't stick, won't burn your baked goods" angle pretty quickly. But a few just couldn't seem to wrap their brains around it. For instance, once I was giving the dimensions of our jelly roll pan, which measured 10 by 15 inches. At that point a woman listening to my spiel piped in with "I'm looking for a 15-by-10 pan."

I had to think about that one for a moment. Then I explained, as slowly as possible, that our pan measured 10 by 15, which was exactly the same as 15 by 10. The only difference was that I put the 10 before the 15. "No," the woman said. "There's a difference." She kept insisting they were different, though of course she couldn't spell out how. This got so embarrassing that the other ladies waiting in line started to turn away. I kept at it, trying to help this woman understand that we were arguing semantics and nothing else. But she wasn't buying it. Finally, I simply had to walk away. Though I couldn't help her, I sincerely hope that somehow, somewhere, maybe in some alternate universe she found what she needed.

Compared to the work involved with getting to shows, setting up the booth, and selling the pans, the occasional oddball wasn't that big a deal. The reason I didn't mind going to so much trouble was that a well-run booth could bring in thousands of dollars for the company. Since our average individual sale was around $20, that meant we had to keep hopping. At the Nutcracker Market in Houston, we set a one-day sales record. I remember I served as a runner, dragging a dolly out to the truck, loading up, taking it back to the booth, offloading, and then doing it all over again. I could barely keep up. But although it was exhausting, thinking about the bottom line helped keep me going.

Not that hard work and good salesmanship were always the answer. Sometimes luck mattered, too. I remember one guy who made a small fortune selling pussy willow twigs for $5 a bundle. It seemed as if every person at that particular show carried one of those bundles. Eventually I found out that each day he "replenished his inventory" by stopping at a big pond and cutting a fresh supply. So while we were selling a product that took time, labor, and precious capital to create, he was chopping down weeds and getting rich. It was perplexing; yet in a twisted way, it was wonderful. Kind of like the pet rock craze. Only in America.

Family Affair

[*Bette*]

Some of my fondest memories are of the Parke County Covered Bridge Festival, which takes place every October in the communities just north of Doughmakers' hometown of Terre Haute. It's a classic heartland harvest celebration, with thousands of people spending ten crisp, cloudless fall days taking in the vibrant foliage, enjoying special concerts, and touring the county's thirty-two beautifully restored covered bridges (so many that the area proclaims itself "the covered bridge capital of the world").

For the past few years we've marked this event in our own way: by setting up three Doughmakers booths around the county, all staffed by family members. I've been lucky enough to handle the booth located one block east of the courthouse square in the tiny town of Rockville. We call that booth "the Taj Mahal" because there's a bathroom—a fantastic luxury for trade show people. And if someone purchases a lot of metal, they can pull their car right up next to us and pick it up. Now that's *true* luxury.

Each evening after a long day of selling, Brooks would fix dinner, and we'd gather around my dining room table to compare notes, tell war stories, and decide who made the most money that day. We'd keep careful track and have a friendly competition to see who got the most sales.

The festival creates a lot of warm personal memories along with another page of Doughmakers lore. In our family it's not uncommon for the line between the personal and the professional to blur like this. When the Cuvelier clan gets together, a backyard cookout may turn into a business meeting, or a confab in the big conference room at headquarters may include a discussion about a child's case of the sniffles. That's pretty unusual for most companies, but not for us. Every day at the office is like a family reunion with spreadsheets.

The company was meant to be a family affair, but it didn't start quite as big a one. Originally it was Diane and me plus, for a little while during the early days, our sister Barb. Although at the time she worked as a real estate agent in Orlando, she found time to help us with all sorts of start-up issues, including publicity. She designed some of the first Doughmakers promotional cards and brochures before bowing out to go into business with her husband, who owns a photo studio.

When it came to hands-on, day-to-day labor, at the beginning it was pretty much Diane and me, with Brooks purchasing raw aluminum and acting as adviser (when he had time). Back then that was all the people power we needed to keep tiny Doughmakers humming. But we got big quick—quicker than any of us dared dream. Remember how I couldn't imagine making $30,000 in our first year? Well, I was right. That was nowhere near the figure we netted. We did $80,000 instead. In our second year we sold $250,000, and in our third year, $600,000.

Soon Brooks became much more than an informal adviser; he was our chief operating officer and a full partner. But as our staff and our prospects grew, Diane and I started thinking even bigger. At that point we were so sure Doughmakers was going to make it, we wanted to share it with the entire family. We wanted everybody to come and join us. However, we concentrated our attention on our brothers Rich and Clay. One of them, we felt, would benefit from moving to Terre Haute. The other was already there.

Our first "acquisition" was Clay and his wife, Debbie. Frankly, it made me a little nervous because he already had such a nice life. He was a self-employed carpenter in upstate New York, and Debbie worked in a hospital. Their kids were deeply involved in hockey—to the point where if they weren't working, sleeping, or in school, they were either watching or playing in a game.

At the time we started thinking about our brother, Diane and I were still making pans by hand and driving from one end of the country to the other selling them. Actually, Clay was sort of in the same boat. His carpentry business was so all-consuming that he had very little free time. Plus, he's one of those guys who always has to be doing something. Clay's an avid deer hunter, so when he visited us, I would buy him deer-hunting videos and literally order him to sit down in front of the TV and watch. It was pretty much the only way to get him to relax. Except he didn't relax. Mr. Type A would sit on the edge of the couch, and if something exciting happened, he'd leap out of his seat and jump up and down. I can't imagine what he must have been like at his kids' hockey games.

That energy, we felt, would add an important ingredient to the Doughmakers mix. Forget about hammering nails. We wanted him selling pans.

One day during the summer of 1999, Brooks visited Clay and Debbie in New York. He asked them to come to Terre Haute, look over the operation, and hear what we had to offer. So they made the journey, weighed their options, and—in spite of the fact that there is no hockey to speak of here in the Midwest—signed on. The two of them threw all their efforts into Doughmakers. Clay would work until 8 or 9 P.M. if needed and go to shows whenever and wherever necessary. As for Debbie, our manager of customer service, she's what being a team player is all about. If you have a lot of work to do, the first words out of her mouth are "What can I help you with?" That's always a wonderful thing to hear.

Our other brother, Rich, came aboard in the fall of that same year. Unlike Clay, who had to uproot his entire existence, Rich's life wasn't disrupted at all. Having worked for years at Specialty Blanks and consistently taking honors as their number one salesman, he already lived in Terre Haute. As a matter of fact, Diane could probably throw a rock from her backyard and hit his house.

When Specialty Blanks was sold, Rich moved to California to explore starting his own business. Over the years he had made many friends in the automotive world, and Rich felt there was room in the custom wheel industry for another player. Unfortunately for him, and fortunately for us, his plans didn't come together. Although living in southern California has its up side for a young guy in his thirties, life out there can be a challenge. Two hours a day on the 405 freeway along with the high cost of living were enough to drive Rich back to Indiana—and right back to his sisters who were waiting with open arms. Bette and I knew his sales skills, his energy, and his focus were exactly what we needed at Doughmakers. But he was having none of it. It was just *bakeware*, he said, and it looked like it was made in a garage. He was skeptical of the sales we were doing, and he doubted our product had much of a future be-yond shows and fund-raising.

By that time Clay was already on the payroll and knee-deep in our plan to recruit his little brother. During the summer he talked Rich into going with him to one of our shows. They hit the road together, and Rich, who is the un-challenged salesman extraordinaire, was amazed to see how good Clay, an ex-carpenter, had become at moving product. It was a thing to behold. Clay worked the room, bantering like a professional and selling pans like crazy.

Something else impressed Rich. Even though we were still in the early years, the first Doughheads had already appeared. As these satisfied customers started turning up at the booth and offering words of support, a light went on in my brother's head. "This is a salesman's dream," Rich told us later. "To have people come up and give testimonials about the product. They're selling it all by themselves." From that day forward he was part of our team. Clay is now di-rector of operations, and Rich heads up sales.

They also do shows together, where they get a reaction that is decidedly dif-ferent from either Diane or me. Every time they come home, they're usually carrying several plates of cookies or other baked items. When we ask them how they always get cookies, they say, "Well, the ladies just say they're going to make us some." Personally, I think some of the Doughheads just have crushes on them.

Or maybe it's some kind of barter deal. If a potential customer tells them about a recipe she's famous for, my brothers will sometimes say, "Make one of those for me next year, and I'll give you a pan of your choice." Which is fine, I guess, except that often as not Diane or some other member of the team winds up staffing that event the next year. One time at a Cleveland show a woman came up to me with a note from Rich that read, "If you bring me a nut roll, you can have anything you want." *Anything you want?* Diane and I had no idea what that meant, though we had visions of the woman asking for the truck we'd ar-rived in. Fortunately, she was really nice. All she wanted was one pan.

Once this approach almost backfired on Clay and Rich. They were working an incredibly busy show in Minneapolis, and in the midst of it all, they told a lady and her two young daughters that they guaranteed she'd love our pans and that nothing would ever stick to them. Well, the next day the guys were man-ning the booth when they spotted this woman coming toward them carrying a clear plastic bag containing a baking sheet with burned cookies stuck to it. They both broke out in a sweat. As it turned out, the woman had brought one

Richard, Donnie, and Clay with Mom.

of her pans from home to show how useless it was. One of her daughters was carrying a plate of cookies flawlessly baked on our pan. They couldn't say enough good things. They even brought a camera so they could take a picture of my brothers with the two little girls.

After signing on our siblings, we also lured Mom into the fold. In 2003 we moved her up from Florida, and now she's a permanent fixture around Dough-makers. But even before that, when she would come to town for six months out of the year, she'd be in the office most days helping with mailings, baking cook-ies for special events, and doing whatever else she wanted to do. She's so proud of the whole operation. She's our number one cheerleader and not a bad sales-person, either. During our first years in business when she was still in Florida, she would make an annual summer pilgrimage to Rochester. Before she started the drive, she would fill her trunk with Doughmakers bakeware. On her way north she visited friends and, like any good Doughhead, passed out pans and talked up the product. Her efforts encouraged more than a few organizations to buy our wares for their fund-raisers.

Truthfully, Mom was pretty hands-on from the time we first started out. She actually went to many shows with Diane and me. Though she was the only person who could violate the "no sitting in the booth" rule with impunity, she always pulled her weight. She helped arrange things in the booths, and when business got hot and heavy, she was right there beside us, talking up the pans and selling them.

Mom doesn't do the shows anymore, but she's still trying to make the world a better place through bakeware. Last year when her church in Florida overextended itself during a building project, she decided to help. Using a $600 tax refund check she received from the government, she purchased $600 worth of pans from the company, wholesale. Then she sold them at retail, doubled her money, and gave it to the church.

It took a few years, but now most of us are under one roof. Yes, we understand how odd this is. Lots of people, if placed in our position, might want anybody but relatives for business partners. But while blood and money can be an explosive mix for some, it hasn't been for us. Our philosophy is, if we're hugely successful, great. If we aren't, let's make sure we all get out of this as friends because it would be devastating if we started fighting over money.

Not that there's much chance of that. The Cuvelier kids battle over who gets the last meatball at dinner and who rides shotgun in the car, but money? Never.

Word of Mouth

[*Bette*]

Throughout its history, Doughmakers has faced three major tasks: making the pans, selling the pans, and, telling the world about the pans.

Sometimes, when circumstances dictate, we use ploys and wiles that only a baking company can conjure up. At big, important trade shows where buyers for national retail chains roam the aisles, we offer far more than a speech about our product. We haul in a full-size oven and bake fresh pies, breads, and cookies. Our sales reps love this. As a matter of fact, if they're bringing someone particularly important by the booth, they may ask us ahead of time to make one of that person's favorites. So I guess you could say we're putting our money where our mouths are.

For other functions, such as in-store demonstrations, we fall back on a little something we like to call Show Cookies. Loaded with oatmeal, chocolate chips, coconut, and nuts, they're invariably a hit wherever we go. But I'll let you in on a little secret: Though the recipes for cookies in this book are made from scratch, occasionally circumstances on the road force us to take a short-cut. If necessary, we'll purchase bags of Betty Crocker oatmeal chocolate chip cookie mix and doctor them up with all sorts of extra ingredients. And without fail, people always ask for our on-the-road "show cookie" recipe.

Of course, in most places we don't have to rely on free goodies; the pans are their own best advertisements. That's one of the reasons we decided to visit so many trade shows and fairs. They could be very profitable, but they were also excellent places to build grass roots name recognition. We could meet with thousands of buyers each day, teach them about our product, and show them the Doughmakers advantage.

But I'll share with you another little secret. When we hit the fairs and shows, we don't just hand out information about our products. We collect it, too, and I always pepper customers with questions. like "What kind of bakeware are you using now?" "Are you satisfied with it?" "How could it be improved?" For years I was a one-woman market research department, gathering opinions one consumer at a time.

That data comes in handy whenever we develop a new addition to the Doughmakers line. It was instrumental in the creation of the piecrust protector that is sold with our pie pans. For any baking novices out there, a crust protector is the metal ring that fits over the exposed crust around the edge of a pie, keeping it from burning during baking. Retailers around the country reported that these doodads were big sellers. However, our customers said they all had one major drawback: They often didn't fit their pie pans properly. Our solution was to offer a customized model with every Doughmakers pie pan so that a proper fit was guaranteed.

That sort of face-to-face feedback is incorporated into almost everything we make. The handles on our pans, even the extra depth in our cake pans, are all there because the Doughheads wanted them. And the only reason we knew they wanted them was that we asked and then we listened.

Talking to customers one at a time built up a loyal following, but it wasn't the way to build a *mass* following. For that we needed publicity. But how does a tiny manufacturer get the attention of major media outlets? In our case we did it by turning to our trusty first employee, Joyce McClelland. She landed our big publicity breakthrough, one that is still paying dividends.

Joyce was and remains an avid fan of *Taste of Home*—a subscriber-only magazine that publishes, among other things, recipes sent in by its readers. It has some 5 million subscribers, most of whom, like Joyce, read each new issue from cover to cover. One day she told Diane and me about a section called "Cooking Up a Business," which profiled home-based companies centered around cooking or baking. Well, our business was still pretty much home-based. We'd only just moved out of our garage, and our "corporate office" was my oldest daughter's upstairs bedroom. Doughmakers seemed like a perfect candidate.

"How about if I write *Taste of Home* a letter telling them about us and send them a couple of pans?" Joyce asked. It sounded great, so that fall we dispatched a letter and a couple of cookie sheets. And we didn't hear a word back—that is, until the next spring. One day I came back to the house after lunch and found Joyce dancing around downstairs, yelling, "They called! They called!"

And not just anyone, but the editor of *Taste of Home* herself. She said they'd received the pans months earlier, shelved them someplace, and forgot about them—until they started a massive cookie recipe contest that brought in some thirty thousand reader entries. Naturally their test kitchen, which was charged with baking and sampling hundreds of the most promising candidates, was overwhelmed. They put every cookie sheet they could find into use, including ours.

"The home economists went crazy over them," the editor told us. "Can you send us some more?"

Of course we said yes. We sent an entire case free of charge. Two weeks later we received a call from The Country Store, a catalog for kitchen products that is affiliated with *Taste of Home.* In no time we landed an order for 755 of our "grand" cookie sheets, plus 755 of our "mega" sheets. Then the magazine itself did a story about our company, and we got our first big burst of national exposure.

A few years ago I finally had a chance to stop by the magazine's offices and visit their test kitchen. It was a wonderful trip. Everyone treated us like royalty. But when the home economists said they wanted to show me the original pans we'd sent, I got a little worried. I wondered how they would look after years of extremely heavy use. To my immense relief, however, they were still bright and shiny after thousands of passes through their ovens.

That was a big break. And even though we've been profiled in lots of magazines and newspapers since, we still haven't lost our desire to talk to people in person. That's one of the reasons Diane and I started offering baking classes around the country. In the beginning it was sort of a stretch for me, because even though I've talked to thousands of people one-on-one, speaking in front of a group was something else. The first time I taught a class, our vice president of marketing, William Wagnon (author of several of this book's pizza recipes), went with me. I figured he was my safety net. William is an Episcopal priest who came to Terre Haute when his wife, also a pastor, was called to serve a

Diane, Bette, Barbara, Jean, and Bev.

church here. He knows how to engage a crowd, so I imagined that if I made a complete mess of things, he could step in with some soothing words and make everything better.

That first class took place at a Cincinnati-area store. It turned out to be a very tough crowd, for good reason. It took place the week after terrorists attacked the World Trade Center and the Pentagon, on September 11, 2001. Everybody's emotions were on edge, including mine. My program was called "Baking Up Memories." William and I discussed it on the drive over, and we decided the best approach would be honesty: to say that it was an emotional time for us, too, but that at moments like these, it was important to connect with the people who are important to you, such as family. And a great way to connect with family is to spend time in the kitchen together.

So, naturally, I sprinkled the presentation with stories of my own family—which made me nostalgic, which made me emotional, which made me start crying, right there in front of a roomful of strangers.

I guess it was becoming clear that I wasn't a professional chef demonstrating a fancy technique. Our reasons for baking and the way we bake come from different places. We were being ourselves and not putting on airs. And with that, the women in the class also opened up, and we had a grand time.

Our reviews on the comment cards were good, and when it was over, I had to admit I had fun. So William signed me up—and later Diane—for more and more presentations. I still like them—once I get there. Remember, I was on my way to one of those sessions when I got caught in a Rocky Mountain blizzard.

In the summer of 1999, after about two and a half years of doing shows and selling the product face-to-face, we began to think seriously about offering it through stores—partly out of loyalty to our Doughheads. Customers who bought at a show would call us and want to know where they could get more. Somehow saying "Wait until we come back next year" wasn't going to work.

Even more troubling were the retail stores that asked to carry our "line." Truthfully, there was no line. Two cookie sheets, a pizza pan, and a sheet cake pan were all we had. We did start shipping to a few stores, but we were hardly prepared for retail. We had to learn over a span of eighteen months everything that went into launching a brand. We had to create packaging and brochures and point-of-purchase displays. We had to figure out what UPC codes were and how to produce them. We had to create systems for shipping, accounting, and increased production. We had to get serious about personnel policies, benefits, and plant safety.

Once again, though, hard work and word of mouth served us well. We debuted our retail line in January 2001 at the International Housewares Show in Chicago. Our booth wasn't in the most high-profile spot, but we still got swarmed. Store owners who had heard or been told by customers about our products actually sought us out. It went far beyond anything we thought we'd get—primarily, I think, because store owners were excited to see something truly new in bakeware.

Even with our success in the retail market, we still go to dozens of shows every year, and we still talk to thousands of bakers about their likes and dislikes. In addition to those appearances, I am sometimes asked to speak to groups about entrepreneurship and being a small business owner. Recently I was asked to talk to some doctors' wives, and during the question-and-answer session a woman stood up and said, "I just hope your mom and dad are both alive, because they must be awfully proud of you kids." Well, I had to tell her that my dad had passed away, and then, of course, the tears started falling.

I think we all wish that Dad could have been here for this. Back when

Brooks sold Specialty Blanks, we tried to help Mom in various ways. I thought at the time that I wished Dad was still around so we could do something for him, too. For instance, it wasn't until all of us kids left home and there was some spare cash lying around that he was able to indulge his love of clothes. He never had a chance to get a really nice wardrobe until we moved out. After that, Mom said she couldn't keep him out of the mall.

But I try not to worry too much about that. I'm sure that he's still watching over us. Maybe he can even read our press clippings up there.

Trouble

[*Diane*]

Doughmakers has made me a stronger woman than I ever was before—literally stronger because I've hauled boxes of metal back and forth across the country for the past seven years. At the biggest shows we'd load, unload, and reload maybe 15,000 pounds of aluminum.

Doughmakers has also developed in me a strength of will that I never had before. The old Diane was so emotionally helpless that I couldn't imagine being out on my own. But during my years on the road for this company, I had to overcome obstacles ranging from flat tires to stolen money to spilled lattes. I became such a can-do person that the former Diane wouldn't recognize herself.

But in 2003 a private tragedy showed me a new kind of strength, a strength of faith. At the beginning of that year I took an extended hiatus from road work and from most of my other duties as well. I had dreamed of getting some down time for quite a while. The year-round grind was starting to get to me. I'd spend the summer roasting in booths at outdoor fairs. Then the fall shows would kick the schedule into high gear, building to the frantic pre-Christmas rush. During those long, long trips I missed my kids terribly. Of course, they were safe with my brothers and sisters, but I still felt like a major schmuck for not being there myself. And yet what could I do? I was part of a company.

Everyone else was doing what they were supposed to do, I'd tell myself, so why couldn't I?

But this kind of thinking doesn't cut it with kids. For a while mentioning Doughmakers to my children was akin to bringing up the Antichrist. They didn't want to hear about it because as far as they were concerned, it was the thing that kept their mom away. So I explained again and again that it wasn't really a choice between my being home all day or away on the road selling bakeware. It was a choice between my being gone all day and many nights working at go-nowhere jobs or my being gone working on something that could provide us with a future. As Emily and Tommy have gotten older, they see the logic in what I was saying.

The emotional burden slowly got better, too, but the physical hardships didn't. If anything, they got worse. Sure, I had more staff, but there were more shows to do. At the end of the 2002 holiday season I felt, as I usually did at that time, that I needed a long, long break. Well, I was about to get one, but not on my terms.

In January 2003 I got sick. I had just returned from Florida where I'd helped Mom pack up to move to Terre Haute. My illness started with just a cough, some shortness of breath, and some sluggishness. But the fatigue slowly got worse. Just walking from the house to my car left me winded, so winded that I had to sit for a few minutes in the driver's seat to recover.

For some reason I got it into my head that I had pneumonia. I went to a doctor who suspected the same and prescribed an antibiotic. It didn't help, so I asked for an inhaler. It didn't have the slightest effect on my shortness of breath. By the time I finished the antibiotics, I was sicker than ever. For several more days I flailed around, trying to decide what was wrong and what I should do. I think my indecision was due to the ever-decreasing amount of oxygen reaching my brain. I was so fuzzy, I couldn't put two and two together and realize I was in big trouble. But that weekend Mom stopped over, took one look at me, called Bette, and announced that I was going to the doctor immediately.

Bette and Mom took me to an emergency-medicine clinic. The doctor on duty knew instantly that I was full of fluid. He recommended that I go to a hospital emergency room to have some of it drained off. He also said something like "I'm hearing something funny with your heart."

That pronouncement scared me, but so did the emergency room we went to. I've never seen so many coughing, snot-filled people in one place in my life. If you didn't arrive sick, you could leave that way. I wearily took a seat and picked up a *Reader's Digest*. I started reading, of all things, an article about people who contracted horrible diseases while sitting in emergency rooms. It struck me as funny, so I laughed—and kept laughing. Here I was in the midst of some sort of medical crisis, and I'd contracted a case of the giggles.

It was all downhill, decorum-wise, from there. After an hour's wait I finally got to see a doctor and was given a chest X ray. Afterward, Bette and I continued carrying on about the *Reader's Digest* article. Then we noticed my doctor examining an X ray at the nurses' station all the way down the hall. It was impossible to tell from that distance, but Bette was absolutely sure it was my X ray. So I said, "Can you read it from thirty paces? I'm sure you can. If anybody can read a chest X ray from thirty feet, it's you."

So Bette squinted her eyes theatrically and said, "It's kind of hard, but . . ."

I told her to just walk up to the doctor and ask if he concurred with her diagnosis. More laughter—or, in my case, a weird hyena-like wheeze. I laughed so hard I couldn't breathe, and I was on the verge of losing bladder control. I figured that would present a really interesting set of symptoms for the doctor to mull over. Helplessly, I waved Bette toward the door, trying to get her to leave. I couldn't even look at her without laughing (and wheezing). But then I noticed that she had her legs crossed. She couldn't go anywhere because she was about to have an accident, too.

Finally she and Mom collected themselves and left. The doctor couldn't tell me much about my condition, so he kept me at the hospital overnight for observation. It wasn't until the next day, after a battery of tests, that I got the bad news. I didn't have pneumonia, I had ischemic cardiomyopathy which was causing congestive heart failure.

The doctor didn't beat around the bush. "It's not good at all," he told me. "It's really bad." And then he laid it all out for me: A virus of some sort—we'll never know what—had invaded my body and damaged my heart, probably irreparably. It was dramatically enlarged and pumping at only 16 percent capacity (60 to 65 percent is normal), and I was now considered a possible candidate for a transplant.

I was lucky I got help when I did. At the hospital they drained 18 pounds of excess fluid out of me. For days I had been lying around the house on my back, literally drowning in all that liquid. I'd also had countless episodes in which I found myself suddenly gasping for air. I learned that those occurred when my heart went into fibrillation—an irregular rhythm—which could have ended in cardiac arrest and sudden death.

My family tried to put up a brave front, but, let's face it, we're criers, boys and girls alike. Bette and Clay were at the hospital the day I was getting tested, and they got the news at about the same time I did. Apparently they were told that I was in really bad shape, that the next couple of days would be critical, and that there was a pretty decent chance I wouldn't make it. Then, immediately after dropping the bomb on them, the doctors let them visit me.

The minute I saw their faces, I knew they'd been crying. "I know," I told them. "My heart is a piece of junk."

That day, after I felt a little better, the two of them wheeled me down to the hospital atrium. I told them I had to make a will, so we called a lawyer and I told her exactly what to do. While I was still in the hospital, we drew up the document, complete with instructions for the guardianship of my kids— because at that time no one was sure I'd be coming home, and I sure as hell didn't want them going back to their father.

Well, my life didn't end, but everything about it changed. I was hospitalized for ten days. When I came out, I had a pacemaker/defibrillator to control my irregular heartbeat, more pills than I could count, and instructions to lose weight and change my lifestyle so I could get on the transplant list.

I was forty-three years old, and I was probably going to have to get a new heart that at most was expected to last about sixteen years.

I had to quit so many things, it wasn't even funny. Cigarettes and alcohol were out. So were the three triple lattes I downed each day from my new Day-Glo orange *Francis! Francis!* espresso machine (*Francis!* I will miss you). And I had to cut out salt, because people with congestive heart failure shouldn't do anything to increase the buildup of internal fluids. I figured the only fun thing I could still do was lie in the sun by a pool. But then I found out during a recuperation trip to Florida—with my sister Bev, a nurse, and her husband, Norm, a doctor—that my medications made me photosensitive. I broke out in sun poisoning!

After that I was the mayor of No Fun Town. Population: me.

I'm not complaining. I'm blessed. I still have my children, my family, and my life. When I first got sick, they all rallied around—to the point where after a while I had to kick them out of my hospital room. There could be fifteen people in there for days on end. At dinner time they'd get into arguments over how many should stay behind with me. I finally told them, "Can I have an hour to myself, please? I beg you." But that's just the way they are. They like to help.

During those dark days no one went further out of his way than my old preteen nemesis, Donnie. He flew in from New York and stayed with me for several nights in the hospital. Then he hung around for a week after I went home and took care of me. It was a super sweet thing to do, especially since he has a wife and four children at home. But he's a total giver. It was so nice to have him there. He was Mr. Gourmet Cook, really trying to help me find things to eat on my strict, low-salt diet. He made his special Chicken French using a low-sodium, low-fat recipe he developed just for me. In addition to cooking, he cleaned the house and did laundry. I'll never forget that.

After he'd been gone for a few days and the house was falling back into its usual chaos, Emily, my daughter, was making breakfast for herself. I heard this funny-sad cry from the kitchen. "My people are gone!" she said. "I just don't know what I'm going to do." Not to worry, though. Aunt Bev showed up a few days later to pick up the slack.

Once I got out of the hospital I wasn't in any pain, but I was a shadow of my former self. The drugs I had to take made me incredibly tired, and my damaged heart made me as weak as a kitten. For the foreseeable future, my Doughmakers road work seemed to be over. Remember how I could rustle up a thousand pounds of bakeware, then drive halfway across the country? After the heart problem, I would start gasping halfway through a trip to the grocery store.

Although I was laid up, I still wanted to keep current on what was going on in the big, wide world. Jason Lloyd, a longtime Doughmakers employee and one of my partners on the road, sent me postcards from various ports of call. I also received cards and flowers from some of the booth operators I'd known for years, plus notes from more than a few Doughheads. It's nice to know you're missed. At one point Jason even made me an offer I almost couldn't refuse. "I'll do all the work," he said, "if you'll just come on the road with us and sit there." It was a sweet idea, but, sorry, no sitting in the booth.

Instead I did my sitting at home. During my weeks of convalescence I had a lot of time to mull things over. Sometimes I'd think about what a huge difference Doughmakers had made in my life. Before it came along, I was working two jobs and barely making ends meet. Now I have a good salary and a nice three-bedroom home that is perfect for the kids and me. I'm close to the plant, and Rich and Clay live within walking distance—one directly behind and one just a block down the road.

Things certainly could have turned out differently. On that recuperation trip to Florida I saw some of my friends from that era of my life. I came away thinking how lucky I was. I thank God that I'm up here with my family. They did such a good job when I was out on the road of helping to raise my kids. Many of my friends' children got involved in drugs, drinking, and all kinds of horrible things. I might have been in exactly the same boat had I not gotten this opportunity.

Of course, I owe a lot to Bette and Brooks. They don't talk about it much, but the fact is, when they started Doughmakers, they were already financially set. No one would have blamed them if they had simply retired, moved some-place warm, and enjoyed themselves for the rest of their lives. Instead, Bette started her own business and made a point of bringing in her kid sister as a part-ner. She set aside her own happiness and plunged into Doughmakers, hoping to make it a success but also hoping to make a success out of me.

Months after the attack I returned to work on a very limited schedule. My biggest projects were writing this book with Bette and also testing the recipes we've included. Unfortunately (for me), someone else had to sample them. Things like Apple Harvest Danish (page 130) and Lemon Chess Pie (page 230) just don't fit into my super-restrictive diet. At the time I figured my days on the road were history. I saw myself puttering around the office, assisting with sales and PR, but leaving more strenuous tasks to others—because the simple fact is that people with my kind of heart damage just don't get better. Or do they?

Ever since I became ill I've been told that the chances of recovery were one in a million. Well, I just might be that one. In May 2003, three months after I got sick, I had an echocardiogram to test how well my heart was working. The doctors were amazed to learn that my ejection fraction (the amount of blood pumped through my heart) had risen from 16 percent to a little more than 30 percent. If that efficiency rises to 55/60, I will for all intents and purposes be back to normal and off the transplant list for good.

The doctor said I may be one of the handful of lucky people who are struck by viruses that don't do permanent damage. In most cases there is no real hope, but making such a significant improvement in such a short time bodes well for the future. Within a year I should know if I will have a full recovery. That bog-gles the mind. Just a little while ago "recovery" was a word I didn't dare think about.

I also didn't dare think about going back on the road—until the summer of 2003 when I decided I felt good enough to give it a try. Bette and I hit a couple of the smaller shows as a test run, and then in late August I tackled my baptism by fire, the infamous Minnesota State Fair. It was just as hot, sweaty, and crowded as usual, but it was so good to be working again, meeting old friends, and talking with the Doughheads that it felt like a week at Disney World.

Of course it wasn't *exactly* like old times. Although I felt much better than I had only a few months earlier, I still wasn't the person I was. My doctor told me not to lift more than 30 pounds at a time, and Bette made me promise to rest whenever I felt tired. So pushing metal-laden dollies up steep ramps was out of the question. Also, whenever I felt tired, I excused myself from the booth and took a nap in our air-conditioned truck. And finally, though it galls me to say it, I kept a stool in the booth where I could sit down.

One other thing has changed: my outlook. During my presickness road trips I tended to let the heat, the confusion, and even the people around me get under my skin. Also, I thought the fate of the world hinged on each day's sales figures. Now, minor annoyances just roll off my back. There's nothing like facing a true life-or-death crisis to put all those run-of-the-mill difficulties into perspective.

As this manuscript is being polished, I'm handling two or three shows each month, doing all the work my condition will allow. I intend to stick with it for as long as possible—maybe for good. I'm gradually gaining energy, though my blood pressure-lowering medications still make me sluggish. But at least now I have hope, and that is truly a miracle drug.

The Future

[*Bette*]

One of the last big Doughmakers projects that Diane worked on before she got sick was our 2002 Christmas warehouse sale. These gatherings are pretty novel events because instead of us going to the Doughheads, the Doughheads come to us.

Do they ever. The warehouse shows, held on the factory floor of our Terre Haute headquarters, draw hundreds upon hundreds of baking fans. On this particular occasion a line of customers nearly ringed the building on opening day. You'd have thought a rock band was playing inside.

But what we offered was even more exciting to hard-core bakers—table after table stacked high with specially priced Doughmakers items plus extra specially priced factory seconds. If a pan had, say, an inconsequential ding on its underside, that meant some lucky customer was going to take it home for a song. And don't think our loyal Doughheads didn't know this. When the sale began, our warehouse and factory, which is a big area, were packed with so many people—some pulling shopping carts laden with enough metal to build a battleship—that at times you couldn't raise your arms from your sides.

Getting bargains is fun, but we wanted to make the sale even more special for our loyal customers, so Diane, Mom, a host of volunteers, and I baked literally hundreds of cookies to pass out to shoppers. In preparation we filled an entire industrial freezer with chocolate chip cookies (a generic recipe), Carmelitas (see page 80), and Swedish Red Lips (see page 191). But by the end of the first night we'd run through every single one. And the sale had three more days to go!

Somehow we had to make enough cookies to keep up with demand. That night we tried to hash out some way to create the greatest number in the least amount of time. We decided to make one of the quickest of all dessert treats, the bar cookie. The next morning we all showed up at the test kitchen at 5 A.M., broke out our massive sheet cake pans, lined them with parchment paper, and then filled them with oatmeal chocolate chip cookie dough, which we produced by the dozens of pounds in a huge mixer.

The laden trays were slammed into the oven, then pulled out and allowed to rest for ten minutes. The whole works—basically one massive cookie—was then pulled out using the parchment paper. Those great masses of gooey goodness were hustled to a nearby conference room that was transformed into a cooling/cutting station. There they were sliced into manageable bits, plated, and taken out, still warm, to our customers.

This went on for days. And even though there were no fewer than eight people hustling around the kitchen at all times, we could barely keep up. According to our estimates, we baked about five hundred dozen cookies during the sale. We made trip after frenzied trip to a nearby grocery store, grabbing 10-pound bags of chocolate chips and purchasing 25 pounds of flour at one go. Mom spent most of each day cutting up the cookies (which also included lemon bars and peanut butter bars), while Diane and I, both of us covered with flour and chocolate, mixed batter nonstop.

In the midst of all this, a lady poked her head through the window connecting the kitchen to the employee dining area. "Could I ask you girls something?" she said. "Are you going to have a day-old bakery here?"

We all started laughing at the same time. "Ma'am," I said, "we don't have anything in this kitchen that's five minutes old, let alone a day old."

In the end we managed to make enough cookies to keep up with demand. The sweets have always been a tradition during our warehouse sales, but they've become a major production feat of their own. Of course you'd be right to wonder if from a purely economic aspect this was the best use of our time. After all, how often do the CEOs of cereal companies make breakfast for their customers? And have you ever heard of the executives of a fast-food operation taking orders at the drive-thru? Well, making cookies for customers may seem like a small thing to outsiders, but it's important to us. Some of the folks who come to our warehouse sales drive hundreds of miles. Giving them a homemade treat is really the least we can do.

And, in truth, such little things aren't really that little, especially for a company like ours with its unique philosophy. Granted, we're a manufacturing concern with spreadsheets and profit statements and quarterly reports, but we're also built around people. Everyone from phone companies to car makers love to mouth this platitude, but to me—to us—it's a very real sentiment. Consider our history. Our business was conceived not in some corporate think tank but by a family. It started in our garage. We got our story out not with expensive marketing campaigns but by word of mouth. And we built our customer base not by placing our wares in every store in the nation but by selling them face-to-face, one client at a time.

So maybe, given our approach, baking cookies for our faithful Doughheads isn't a distraction. Maybe it's yet another way we set ourselves apart.

I think each warehouse sale is a microcosm of the Doughmakers experience. We work very hard at them, treat people like individuals, and go the extra mile. We're always there for our customers, just as we're always there for our family.

The fact that this is a family business has always been foremost in our minds—especially after Diane got sick. That taught me an important lesson about acceptance. One night while she was sleeping in her hospital bed, I looked at her and thought, "All these years I've been trying to change my sister, and now I thank God that she is who she is." Suddenly I realized that while her temper and independent spirit might occasionally set me on edge, they were the very things that gave her the strength to battle her illness. That was the first time I ever said to myself, "I don't want to change anything about her. I love her just the way she is."

I think that kind of fighting spirit is important when facing any sort of challenge. During the history of Doughmakers we've seen it many times, in many places, in many different people. That willingness to persevere helped turn our tiny company into a national enterprise, and it promises to help us become even more successful in the future.

If I had my druthers, here's how I'd like to see things turn out. First of all, I want Diane to get well. Second, I'd like to see Doughmakers become everything we dreamed it could be, back when the Cuvelier siblings gathered on my back porch and cooked up the idea of a bakeware company. That, to me, isn't measured in market share or profits. It means providing my family and all of our partners and employees with a fun and rewarding place to work and a healthy measure of financial security. That's been the intent from day one. When we started the company, we announced that we'd tithe our profits to charities and provide for generous profit-sharing with employees. I'd love to see each and every one of them get a nice check each year, above and beyond their regular salaries.

As for my own future, I see myself on a beach. Just kidding—though that does sound nice. What I'd really like is for Brooks and me to be surrounded by grandchildren. Our three kids aren't directly involved in the company, but I think they all absorbed the Cuvelier spirit. They're independent, they can keep their heads in crises, and they're great cooks as well. Our oldest, Taylor, who at the age of eighteen months started climbing up on the kitchen counter and mixing things together, is now an expert at meal preparation. We actually bought her a grain mill so she can grind her own wheat to make bread. Wouldn't Grandma Minnie be proud?

It would be great if someday we could step back from the day-to-day operations and spend more time on family matters. That would be particularly wonderful for Brooks, who invested so much of his own money and time getting Doughmakers off the ground. It was so difficult that we might not have done it had we known what was involved. Sometimes we were even tempted to bow out, but our family kept us going. Whenever one of us got discouraged, someone else would step in and lift that person up.

I guess lots of entrepreneurs get discouraged when their best-laid plans are overturned by fate. We can never truly know what the future holds, and it's probably for the best that we can't. Starting a business, like getting married or having a baby, will always be a leap-before-you-look proposition. You have to rely on optimism and have more than a little faith.

Doughmakers Bakeware brought out a unique product at a time when the marketplace for bakeware was looking for a new idea, but there's no substitute for endless hard work and a never-give-up attitude. I would tell those who are thinking of starting or in the middle of starting their own business, that the combination of talents and opportunity that came together for us was different than it will be for you. But you will have your own mix of talent and opportunity, and it can be just as powerful as ours, possibly more so. And also this: Turning a dream into reality is hard—harder, I think, than most people can imagine. But just because it's hard doesn't mean it's not worth doing. And just because you've never done anything like it before, don't think that you can't do it. Seek out people with the knowledge and experience to help you and learn from them. And, most important of all, when you're feeling exhausted and defeated and you think you can't possibly go on, go a little further. There is no substitute for perseverance.

Hang in there, cherish every bit of encouragement you receive along the way, and remember that success takes time. A profitable company, like a loaf of bread, requires patience to make.

Today Doughmakers makes more than a dozen pieces of bakeware, from the original cookie sheets to pie pans to loaf pans. And although our lineup has changed, the way we get them to consumers hasn't. Face-to-face selling seems to be Doughmakers' destiny. For a while we focused on moving up the retail food chain—first by getting our product into smaller stores, then by trying to place it in department stores and "big box" discount chains. But getting there, we realized, meant giving up some of the things that make our offering so special, and losing the ability to accurately communicate the benefits of our product. Would the staffs at big chains take the time to tell the Doughmakers story and explain our advantages over steel and coated bakeware? Highly unlikely.

So we've tempered our goals somewhat, refocusing our efforts on the customers who helped us build the company. We devote ourselves to the individual buyers at fairs and shows, and to the small business owners who run specialty gourmet and grocery stores with the enthusiasm of true Doughheads.

We want to be a face to as many of our buyers as possible—not just a name.

Diane and I plan to help lead that effort. Both of us, for instance, will play a big part in finding new venues to sell Doughmakers. And we'll also be responsible for educating retailers and our own salespeople on how to show consumers just how great our product is.

I think Diane and I (and of course Rich and Clay and all the members of our road teams) have become true masters at selling Doughmakers products. But I sometimes wonder if we could have sold some other item with equal skill. Probably not. I've been told so many times that a really good salesperson can only sell something he or she truly believes in. Otherwise the salesperson can't look a customer in the eye.

It's been my good fortune to sell a product that I believe in and to be surrounded by people who believe in themselves and each other. That faith comes from the Doughmakers staff, my family, and, of course, my mom. One of our biggest joys is that she's seen this company come to life, and one of her biggest joys is seeing us kids working together and having fun while doing it. But then again, I don't think she doubted us for a second. As she likes to say, "I know that if anybody can do this, you kids can do this."

Thanks, Mom.

Recipes

Bar Cookies

Best Ever Brownies

MAKES 24 BROWNIES

Shortly after we launched our retail brand, our pans were tested by Cuisine at Home *magazine. The editors there, especially Sara Ostransky, were—and still are—enthusiastic about our pans and have been very encouraging through the years. This is their best ever brownie recipe, which fits our best ever 9 x 13-inch pan . . . a perfect match.*

—WILLIAM WAGNON, DOUGHMAKERS VICE PRESIDENT OF MARKETING

12 ounces semisweet chocolate,
  broken into small pieces

1½ cups sugar

12 tablespoons (1½ sticks) unsalted
  butter, cut into chunks

1 cup all-purpose flour, plus a little
  extra for flouring the pan

2 teaspoons baking powder

¼ teaspoon salt

¼ cup cocoa, sifted

4 large eggs

1 tablespoon vanilla extract

2 tablespoons crushed instant coffee
  crystals or espresso powder

In a double boiler set to simmer, stir the chocolate, sugar, and butter until melted and smooth. Remove from the heat and cool to room temperature.

Preheat the oven to 350°F.

Grease and flour the bottom and sides of a 9 × 13-inch cake pan. Measure the flour, baking powder, and salt into a mixing bowl and stir to combine. Add the cocoa and stir.

In another bowl, beat the eggs, vanilla, and instant coffee until foamy. Beat in the cooled chocolate mixture. Add about ¼ cup of the flour mixture and fold it into the chocolate. Scrape down the sides of the bowl and repeat until all the flour is added.

Spread the batter evenly in the pan and bake in the center of the oven for 20 to 25 minutes, or until a toothpick inserted in the center comes out almost clean. Remove the brownies from the oven and cool in the pan on a wire rack. Slice them in the pan or turn them onto a wire rack and then invert again onto a cutting board. Slice into 2-inch squares.

▶ *Don't use nonstick cooking spray on your Doughmakers pan. When necessary, grease your pan with solid shortening or butter for best results.*

Carmelitas

MAKES 54 BARS

When I was a youth group leader, I always made cookies for each kid's birthday. And they always wanted my carmelitas. I guess it's what I'm known for. Since I discovered the Doughmakers pans, I won't make my Carmelitas in anything else. —CLARICE DUITS, INDIANAPOLIS, INDIANA

3 cups quick oats

3¾ cups all purpose flour

2¼ cups firmly packed light brown sugar

¾ teaspoon salt

1½ teaspoons baking soda

1 pound and 4 tablespoons butter, melted

2 pounds caramels

8 tablespoons half-and-half

12 ounces semisweet chocolate chip morsels

2 cups chopped pecans (optional)

Preheat the oven to 350°F.

Combine the quick oats, flour, brown sugar, salt, and baking soda in a large bowl and mix thoroughly. Add the melted butter and mix well. Divide the oatmeal mixture in half. Press one half of this dough into an ungreased 13 × 18-inch sheet cake pan. Bake for 10 minutes, until light golden brown.

Meanwhile, melt the caramels and half-and-half in a 2 quart microwave-safe bowl. Microwave on high at 1 minute intervals, stirring in between, until smooth and creamy. Reserve about ⅓ of the caramel mixture and pour the remaining over the oatmeal mixture. Sprinkle the chocolate chips over the caramel. Crumble the remaining oatmeal mixture on top and drizzle with the reserved caramel.

Return the pan to the oven and bake 12 minutes more, until light golden brown. Cool the carmelitas completely before slicing into 2-inch bars. (The bars freeze well for up to 1 month.)

▶ *Lining a pan of bar cookies with parchment paper will make it easier to remove them to the work surface where they can be cut more precisely.*

Carrot Bars

MAKES 36 BARS

This recipe came to us from a loyal customer whom we met at one of the hundreds of consumer shows we have done. These shows give us the chance to meet and talk with people about recipes they love. And when they tell us they love the results they get with our bakeware, we're reminded of why we love what we do! —BETTE

4 eggs, beaten
2 cups sugar
1½ cups vegetable oil
2 cups flour
2 teaspoons baking soda
1 teaspoon salt
1½ teaspoons cinnamon
Three 4-ounce jars of carrot
    baby food

FROSTING:
8 ounces cream cheese
4 tablespoons (½ stick) butter,
    softened
1 teaspoon vanilla extract
3 cups confectioners' sugar
Milk

Preheat the oven to 350°F.

In a large bowl, mix the eggs, sugar, oil, flour, baking soda, salt, and cinnamon. Stir in the baby food. Pour the batter into a greased jelly roll pan (10 × 15-inches). Bake for 15 to 20 minutes, or until a toothpick inserted in the middle comes out clean. Allow the pan to cool on a wire rack.

To prepare the frosting: In a mixer, combine the cream cheese, butter, vanilla, and sugar. Use the milk to thin the frosting to the desired consistency. Spread over the brownies and cut into 2-inch squares.

▶ *Everyone you meet has something to teach you. Get them talking about something they love to do, and they will usually be happy to share what they've learned.*

Chocolate Brownie Bars

MAKES 54 BARS

DOUGH:
1 pound butter, softened
1 cup sugar
1 egg
1 teaspoon vanilla extract
½ teaspoon baking powder
4 cups sifted all-purpose flour

BROWNIE FILLING:
4 cups chocolate chips
⅔ cup firmly packed brown sugar
⅔ cup lightly beaten egg whites
½ dough made above

Preheat the oven to 350°F.

To make the dough, cream together the butter and sugar in a large bowl. Add the egg and vanilla, and stir. Add the baking powder and flour, and beat with an electric mixer for about 3 minutes to make a smooth dough. Chill in the refrigerator for at least 30 minutes.

Press half of the dough into the bottom of an ungreased 13 × 18-inch sheet cake pan, until it covers the entire bottom of the pan and runs up the sides. Pressing with your fingertips is a good way to spread the dough, and it can be spread very thin. Bake for 10 minutes, or until lightly golden.

To prepare the filling: Place the chocolate chips in a large microwave-safe bowl and microwave on high for 30 seconds. Then stir, microwave, and stir again until the chips are melted and have a smooth consistency. Add the sugar, egg whites, and the remaining half of the cookie dough. Beat together with an electric mixer on medium speed until thoroughly combined. Spread the batter carefully over the baked crust.

Bake for 28 to 30 minutes, then let the brownies cool completely in the pan. Cut into 2-inch squares.

▶ *If your baking powder has been on the shelf for a while, test it for freshness: Mix 2 teaspoons of baking powder with 1 cup of hot tap water. If it immediately fizzes and foams, you can use it. If the reaction is delayed or weak, buy a fresh can. We always use Clabber Girl Baking Powder.*

Chocolate-Pineapple Brownies

MAKES 24 BARS

Offered by Patricia Guess, Terre Haute, Indiana.

12 tablespoons (1½ sticks) butter, softened

1½ cups sugar

3 eggs

1 teaspoon vanilla extract

1½ cups sifted flour

½ teaspoon cinnamon

1 teaspoon baking powder

1 cup drained crushed pineapple

Two 1-ounce squares semisweet chocolate, melted

FROSTING:

¾ cup solid vegetable shortening

1 egg white

One 16-ounce box confectioners' sugar

1 tablespoon flour

Dash of salt

1 teaspoon vanilla extract

Milk

Preheat the oven to 325°F. Grease a 9 × 13-inch pan.

Cream the butter and sugar until light. Add the eggs, 1 at a time, beating after each addition. Add the vanilla and beat until fluffy. In a separate bowl, sift together the flour, cinnamon, and baking powder. Add to the creamed mixture. Measure 1 cup of batter into a third bowl, add the pineapple, and blend well. Add the melted chocolate to the batter in the first bowl.

Spread half of the chocolate batter in the prepared pan. Cover with the pineapple batter. Drop the remaining chocolate batter by spoonfuls over the pineapple layer and spread gently over the entire pan. Bake for 45 to 50 minutes, then cool completely.

To make the frosting: Mix together the shortening, egg white, sugar, flour, salt, and vanilla. Add enough milk to make it a nice spreading consistency and beat until fluffy. Spread over the brownies and cut into 2-inch squares.

VARIATION: You can add 1 to 2 tablespoons of cocoa to the frosting ingredients to make chocolate frosting.

▶ *Your butter is "softened" when the stick bends without cracking or breaking. Don't hurry this process with the microwave (as tempting as that is) because the edges will begin to melt before the center is softened.*

Coconut Toffee Bars

MAKES 24 BARS

4 tablespoons butter or margarine, softened

¼ cup solid vegetable shortening

½ cup packed brown sugar

1 cup flour

ALMOND-COCONUT TOPPING:

2 eggs

1 cup packed brown sugar

1 teaspoon vanilla extract

2 tablespoons flour

1 teaspoon baking powder

½ teaspoon salt

1 cup shredded coconut

1 cup chopped almonds

1 cup chocolate chips

Preheat the oven to 350°F.

In a bowl, cream the butter, shortening, and sugar. Blend in the flour. Press the mixture evenly into the bottom of an ungreased 9 × 13-inch cake pan. Bake for 10 minutes, or until lightly golden.

While the cake is baking, prepare the topping: Beat the eggs. Add the sugar, vanilla, flour, baking powder, salt, coconut, and almonds, and stir well.

Spread the partially baked crust with the topping and bake for 25 minutes more, or until the topping is golden brown. Sprinkle with the chocolate chips, allow them to melt, and then spread them evenly over the top. Cool slightly and cut into 2-inch squares.

▶ *If you've ever lost track of which spices you've added to a recipe, try this: Measure the dry ingredients by teaspoon and tablespoon quantities onto a sheet of wax paper in separate piles. You'll see them all before adding any to the mixing bowl.*

Creamy Apple Squares

MAKES 24 BARS

CRUST:

½ pound (2 sticks) cold butter, cut into pieces

2⅓ cups all purpose flour

½ cup confectioners' sugar

2 tablespoons water

FILLING:

16 ounces cream cheese, at room temperature

1 cup sugar

1 egg

1 teaspoon vanilla extract

½ teaspoon almond extract

¼ teaspoon salt

8 cups thinly sliced apples

1 teaspoon cinnamon

3 tablespoons cornstarch

1½ tablespoons lemon juice

TOPPING:

1 cup flour

½ cup sugar

¼ cup firmly packed brown sugar

6 tablespoons butter

GLAZE:

3 tablespoons butter, softened

1 cup confectioners' sugar

2 tablespoons milk

Preheat the oven to 350°F. Line a 9 × 13-inch pan with 2 overlapping pieces of parchment paper that extend up the sides and over the top of the pan by 1 inch.

To make the crust: Using a food processor or a pastry blender, process or cut the butter into the flour and sugar until the mixture is mealy. Add the water and continue mixing until the dough just starts to form a ball. Press into the bottom and ½ inch up the sides of the prepared pan. Bake for about 15 minutes, until the mixture is set and slightly golden. Remove from the oven and set aside.

To make the filling: In a bowl, beat the cream cheese and ½ cup of sugar until smooth. Add the egg, vanilla and almond extracts, and salt, and combine thoroughly. Spread the filling on the prepared crust.

In a large bowl, combine the apples, the remaining ½ cup of sugar, cinnamon, cornstarch, and lemon juice. Spread over the cream cheese layer.

To make the topping: Place flour and sugars in a medium bowl. Cut in the butter until it makes large crumbs. Sprinkle over the filling. Bake for 45 to 55 minutes, until the topping is golden and the apples are tender. Cool completely.

To make the glaze: Mix together thoroughly the butter, sugar, and milk. Drizzle over the bars before cutting into 2-inch squares. Store in the refrigerator in a tightly closed container for up to 5 days.

▶ *Give your small customers the same respect, courtesy, and effort you give your big customers. One day they may be big customers, and they'll remember you for it.*

Fudge Nut Bars

MAKES 3 DOZEN BARS

Offered by Nancy Holgate, West Des Moines, Iowa.

½ pound plus 2 tablespoons
   butter, softened
2 cups brown sugar
2 eggs
4 teaspoons vanilla extract
2½ cups flour
1 teaspoon baking soda
1½ teaspoons salt

3 cups quick-cooking oats
One 12-ounce bag milk chocolate
   chips
1 can sweetened condensed milk
1 cup chopped nuts (optional)

Preheat the oven to 350°F.

In a large bowl, cream together the ½ pound of butter and the sugar. Add the eggs and vanilla, and mix well. Add the flour, baking soda, 1 teaspoon of salt, and the oats, and mix well.

In a double boiler, melt the chocolate chips with the milk, 2 tablespoons of butter, and ½ teaspoon of salt. Stir until smooth, then remove from the heat and add the nuts, if using, and 2 teaspoons of vanilla.

Spread ⅔ of the oatmeal mixture in a 10 x 15-inch jelly roll pan. Pour the melted chocolate mixture over the oat mixture. Sprinkle the remaining oatmeal mixture on top.

Bake for 25 to 30 minutes. Allow to cool in the pan before cutting into 2 inch squares.

▶ *A clean coffee bean grinder can be used for chopping nuts.*

Gold Bars

MAKES 24 BARS

DOUGH:

8 tablespoons (1 stick) butter,
   softened

3 tablespoons sugar

¼ teaspoon salt

1 cup all-purpose flour

1½ cups flaked coconut

1 large egg

1 teaspoon almond extract

FILLING:

1½ cups firmly packed brown sugar

1½ cups coarsely chopped roasted
   macadamia nuts (about 7 ounces)

2 tablespoons all-purpose flour

¾ teaspoon baking powder

¼ teaspoon salt

2 large eggs

1 teaspoon vanilla extract

½ teaspoon almond extract

GLAZE:

¾ cup confectioners' sugar

2 tablespoons fresh lemon juice

Preheat the oven to 350°F. Butter the bottom and sides of a 9 × 13-inch cake pan.

To make the dough: In a large bowl, cream together the butter, sugar, and salt. Add the flour and mix until crumbly. Add the coconut, egg, and almond extract, and stir to form the dough. Press the dough evenly into the bottom of the prepared pan (it will be thin). Bake for 20 to 25 minutes, or until pale golden. Remove from the oven and let cool in the pan on a wire rack.

To make the filling: In a medium bowl, stir together all the ingredients until thoroughly combined. Pour the filling on the crust, spreading it to the edges. Bake for 25 to 30 minutes, or until golden and set. Let cool completely before slicing into 2-inch squares while still in the pan.

To make the glaze: In a medium bowl, stir together the sugar and lemon juice until smooth. Drizzle the glaze back and forth over the bars (see Tip below) and let set.

▶ *To drizzle a glaze, dip a large spoon in the glaze and quickly move it back and forth across the bars, letting the glaze fall off the spoon in a thin ribbon.*

Winter Wonderland Bars

MAKES ABOUT 70 BARS

¾ pound (3 sticks) butter, softened
1 cup confectioners' sugar
3 cups flour
20 ounces white chocolate chips

16 ounces cream cheese, softened
½ cup heavy cream
Crushed peppermint candies
Edible glitter

Preheat the oven to 300°F.

In a large bowl, cream together the butter and sugar. Add the flour and mix together well. Using your fingertips, press the dough into an ungreased 13 × 18-inch sheet cake pan.

Bake for 15 minutes, or until golden brown. Remove from the oven and allow to cool in the pan placed on a wire rack.

Melt the white chocolate chips in a double boiler over medium heat. Remove from the heat and mix in the cream cheese and heavy cream. Spread the mixture over the cooled cookie crust. Chill at least a few hours, and preferably overnight. Decorate with the crushed peppermint candies and edible glitter. Cut into 2-inch squares.

▶ *If you don't have a double boiler, you can place a small metal mixing bowl in a saucepan. Fill the pan with water until at least the bottom quarter of the bowl is covered.*

Pecan Tassies

MAKES 2 DOZEN

White Lily Flour is another company that has been gracious and welcoming to us. Their recipe for pecan tassies is a classic southern treat. These baby pecan pies have the magic of looking complicated but are really easy to make.

One 3-ounce package cream
cheese, softened

¼ pound (1 stick) butter,
softened

1 cup White Lily All-Purpose
Flour, not self-rising

1 large egg

¾ cup packed brown sugar

1 tablespoon butter or margarine,
softened

1 teaspoon vanilla extract

⅛ teaspoon salt

1 cup chopped pecans

In the bowl of an electric mixer, blend the cream cheese and ¼ pound of butter. Stir in the flour just until blended. Wrap this dough and chill it for at least 1 hour and up to 24 hours.

Preheat the oven to 325°F.

While it is still cool, shape the dough into 24 one-inch balls and press one ball into each cup of an ungreased mini-muffin pan. Press the dough up the sides of each cup to make a shallow shell.

In a medium mixing bowl, beat the egg, brown sugar, 1 tablespoon of butter, vanilla, and salt until thoroughly combined. Sprinkle ½ cup of the pecans evenly over the dough in the muffin cups. Add the egg mixture evenly to the cups and sprinkle with the remaining pecans.

Bake for 20 to 25 minutes, or until the fillings are set. Cool in the pans on wire rack.

▶ *Remember to thank your employees for their efforts, and your customers for their business.*

Breads and Rolls

Almond Tea Bread

MAKES 2 LOAVES

Offered by Nancy Holgate, West Des Moines, Iowa.

3 cups sugar

3 eggs

1 cup plus 2 tablespoons oil

3 cups flour

1½ teaspoons salt

1½ teaspoons baking powder

1½ cups milk

1½ teaspoons poppy seeds

2 teaspoons almond flavoring

2 teaspoons butter flavoring

2 teaspoons vanilla extract

¼ cup orange juice

Preheat the oven to 350°F.

In a large bowl, cream together 2¼ cups of sugar, eggs, and oil. In a separate bowl, sift together the flour, salt, and baking powder. Add half of the flour mixture and the milk to the sugar and egg mixture, and stir. Alternate adding the remaining flour mixture and the milk. Add the poppy seeds and 1½ teaspoons each of almond and butter flavorings and vanilla. Beat for 1 to 2 minutes. Pour the batter into two 8½ × 4½-inch loaf pans. Bake for 40 to 50 minutes, or until a tester inserted in the loaves comes out clean.

To prepare the glaze: Bring to a boil the remaining ¾ cup of sugar, the orange juice, and the remaining ½ teaspoon each of the almond and butter flavorings, and the vanilla, stirring constantly. As soon as the mixture boils and the sugar is no longer gritty, remove from the heat. Pour the glaze over the breads while still warm.

▶ *When our company was still very small, we kept track of sales in an old-fashioned ledger book. In the back of that ledger we wrote our prayer concerns and requests, such as "Safe travel for Diane" to a particular show. This helped us keep our business concerns in balance with our family concerns, and reminded us that we were not alone in our efforts.*

Angel Biscuits

MAKES 22 BISCUITS

5 cups all-purpose flour

¼ cup sugar

1 teaspoon baking soda

3 teaspoons baking powder

1 teaspoon salt

1 cup solid vegetable shortening

One ¼-ounce package active dry yeast

2 to 3 tablespoons warm water

2 cups buttermilk

In a large bowl, sift together the flour, sugar, baking soda, baking powder, and salt. Cut in the shortening until coarse crumbs form. In a small bowl, dissolve the yeast in the warm water and add this to the buttermilk in a separate bowl. Add the buttermilk mixture to the flour mixture and stir until all the flour has been moistened. Place the dough in a zippered plastic bag and chill in the refrigerator for at least 2 hours.

When ready to use, preheat the oven to 450°F.

Pinch off about 2 to 3 tablespoons of dough. Roll out or press the dough with your hands until it is about ¼ inch thick, then cut or form into desired shape. Place the biscuits, sides touching, on an ungreased 10 × 14-inch biscuit sheet (see Product List, page 253), and bake for 10 to 12 minutes.

▶ *When selling, remember this: Customers don't want products or features or benefits. They want results and, ultimately, solutions to their problems. Your presentation of your product's features and benefits must always point to these ends. In our case this is better results from your efforts in baking, but at another level we offer the sense of accomplishment at making something yourself and the joy of sharing home-baked goodies with family and friends. We also try to present our product as the antidote to store prepared foods for fast-paced families.*

Southern Buttermilk Biscuits

MAKES 1 DOZEN

2 cups all-purpose flour, plus
    additional for dusting
2 teaspoons baking powder
½ teaspoon baking soda

¾ teaspoon salt
¼ cup solid vegetable shortening,
    cold and cut in 4 to 6 pieces
1 cup buttermilk

Preheat the oven to 450°F.

In the bowl of a mixer or food processor, mix together the flour, baking powder, baking soda, and salt. Add the shortening and pulse until the mixture resembles large coarse crumbs.

Add about ⅓ of the buttermilk and pulse for 3 seconds to begin blending. Repeat 2 more times, until all the buttermilk has been added. If the dough seems firm or dry, add an additional 1 to 2 tablespoons of buttermilk and pulse again.

Sprinkle a work surface with flour and turn the dough out. With your hands, form the dough into a ball. Knead gently for about 5 to 8 strokes, just until it holds together. Pat the dough out to a ½-inch thickness and cut with a 2-inch floured biscuit cutter. Place the biscuits on a greased baking sheet. Bake for 10 to 12 minutes, or until golden brown.

▶ *A light touch when kneading and shaping biscuit dough makes for lighter biscuits. Working the dough more than the bare minimum needed to hold the ingredients together causes gluten to form, which makes the biscuits chewy.*

Bacon Fennel Breadsticks

MAKES ABOUT 12 BREADSTICKS

1 recipe for Quick-Rise or ½ recipe
    for Long-Rise Pizza Dough
    (pages 243 or 241)

6 bacon strips

1 teaspoon fennel

1 teaspoon garlic salt

1 teaspoon freshly ground black
    pepper

1 teaspoon grated Parmesan cheese

2 tablespoons butter, melted

Preheat the oven to 400 °F.

Prepare the pizza dough as directed.

Cut each slice of bacon lengthwise into two long, thin strips. For each breadstick, tear off a bit of the dough and roll it beneath your palms on the work surface, stretching until it is about 12 inches long and ¼ to ½ inch thick. Lay a bacon strip on top of the dough and twist to achieve a barber's pole or candy cane effect.

Crush the fennel with a rolling pin. Place the fennel, garlic salt, pepper, and Parmesan cheese on a sheet of parchment or waxed paper and stir to combine. Roll each breadstick in the spices until coated on all sides. Any remaining dough may be frozen up to 2 weeks and used for breadsticks or pizza.

Arrange the coated breadsticks on a baking sheet or pizza pan and bake for about 15 to 20 minutes. Brush with melted butter before serving.

▶ *We always laugh to ourselves when people say, "It must be great to own your own business because you can set your hours and come and go as you please." The hours of the small business owner are 24/7/365, nothing less.*

Classic White Bread

MAKES 2 LOAVES

2½ cups warm water (105°–110°F)

One ¼-ounce package active dry yeast

1 tablespoon sugar

6 to 7 cups bread flour or unbleached all-purpose flour

1 tablespoon salt

4 tablespoons unsalted butter, at room temperature

Vegetable oil

Pour ½ cup of water into a large mixing bowl. Sprinkle in the yeast and sugar, and whisk to blend. Allow the mixture to rest about 5 minutes, or until the yeast is foamy.

Add the 2 remaining cups of water and mix in about 3½ cups of flour using a dough whisk or wooden spoon. Add the salt and the remaining 3½ cups of flour, a little at a time. Mix well after each addition. As the dough comes together, you can begin to work it with floured hands. Use as little flour as required to form a slightly sticky dough. Add the butter, 1 tablespoon at a time, and work it into the dough with your hands. Turn the dough out onto a lightly floured counter and knead for 10 minutes, or until the dough is smooth. Shape it into a ball.

(Alternately, you can mix the water and yeast by hand in the bowl of a large stand mixer. When the yeast is foamy, add half of the flour and begin to mix on medium-low. Add the salt and the remaining flour, and continue to mix, increasing the speed to medium-high. Then add the butter and mix for 10 minutes. If you mix it this way, knead the dough for only a few strokes as you shape the dough.)

Place the dough in the large oiled bowl. Turn the dough to cover its entire surface with oil. Cover the bowl tightly with plastic wrap and let the dough rest at room temperature until it doubles in size, about 45 minutes to 1 hour.

Butter two 8½ × 4½ inch loaf pans and set them aside.

Punch down the dough and turn it out onto a lightly floured work surface. Divide the dough in half and work with 1 piece at a time. Using the palms of your hands and fingertips or a rolling pin, pat the dough into a large rectangle about 9 inches by 12 inches, with a short side facing you. Starting at the edge away from you, fold down one-third, then bring the far edge down to the near edge, and seal the seam by pinching it. With the sealed seam facing down, put the loaf into a pan. If the loaf is too long, tuck the ends under rather than compress the loaf. Adjust the loaf to get an even shape. Repeat with the other half of the dough.

Brush the tops of the loaves lightly with oil and cover with plastic wrap. Let them rise in a warm place until doubled in size, about 45 minutes. The loaves should rise over the edge of the pan, but if you let them rise too long, the tops may spill over the edge.

Preheat the oven to 375°F. Bake the loaves for 35 to 45 minutes, or until golden brown. Cool them on a wire rack. Make sure they are mostly cool before slicing.

▶ *With all the good, inexpensive bread available from bakeries, you must be making this loaf from scratch because you want to. So go slowly and enjoy it. With each stroke as you knead, think about the people who will enjoy it.*

Clabber Girl
Baking Powder Biscuits

MAKES ABOUT 1 DOZEN 2-INCH BISCUITS

A longtime Terre Haute company, Clabber Girl Baking Powder gave Doughmakers Bakeware an early endorsement as we launched our retail line, which was a tremendous boost to our credibility as a new brand. We'll always be grateful for Clabber Girl's support and encouragement, and the use of their recipes along the way. This recipe is a classic! —BETTE

> 2 cups all-purpose flour
> 1 tablespoon Clabber Girl Baking Powder
> 2 teaspoons sugar
> ½ teaspoon cream of tartar
> ¼ teaspoon salt
> ½ cup solid vegetable shortening, margarine, or butter
> ⅔ cup milk

Preheat the oven to 450°F.

In a medium bowl, stir together the flour, baking powder, sugar, cream of tartar, and salt. Using a pastry blender, cut in the shortening until the mixture resembles coarse crumbs. Make a well in the center and add the milk all at once. Using a fork, stir until just moistened. On a lightly floured surface, knead the dough for 10 to 12 strokes, or until the dough is nearly smooth. Pat or lightly roll the dough to a ½-inch thickness. Cut the dough with a biscuit cutter. Between cuts, dip the biscuit cutter into flour to prevent the dough from sticking to the cutter. Place the biscuits on an ungreased 10 × 14-inch biscuit sheet. Bake for 10 to 12 minutes, or until golden. Serve warm.

VARIATIONS

BUTTERMILK BISCUITS: Prepare as above but with only ¼ teaspoon of baking powder and substitute ¾ cup of buttermilk for the milk.

DROP BISCUITS: Prepare as above except increase the milk to 1 cup. Mix the ingredients with a spoon. Don't knead, roll, or cut them, but drop a tablespoon of dough on a greased biscuit sheet, separating the biscuits by about 1 inch.

CHEESE BISCUITS: Prepare as above except add ½ cup of shredded cheddar cheese to the flour mixture with the milk.

▶ *If you don't have a biscuit cutter, form the dough into round, slightly mounded discs and then cut with a knife into pudgy triangles as you would for scones.*

Cranberry Almond Bread

MAKES 2 LOAVES

1½ teaspoons baking powder
1½ teaspoons baking soda
2½ cups all purpose flour
½ teaspoon salt
½ pound (2 sticks) butter, softened
1½ cups sugar

3 eggs
1½ cups sour cream
1 teaspoon almond extract
One 16-ounce can whole cranberry
  sauce
½ cup chopped almonds

Preheat the oven to 350°F.

Combine the baking powder, baking soda, flour, and salt. Cream together the butter and sugar. Add the eggs and flour mixture alternately with the sour cream. Add the almond extract. In two 8½ × 4½-inch loaf pans, layer the batter alternately with the cranberry sauce. Sprinkle with the almonds and bake for 1 hour.

▶ *Learn to laugh at yourself and with others.*

Doughmakers Soft Pretzels

MAKES ABOUT 1 DOZEN PRETZELS

4½ cups unbleached all-purpose flour

½ cup rye flour or additional all-purpose flour

2 tablespoons malt powder or sugar

Two ¼-ounce packages active dry yeast

1 teaspoon kosher salt

2 tablespoons vegetable oil

1 tablespoon molasses

1½ cups hot water (120° to 130°F)

4 cups warm water

¼ cup baking soda

Pretzel salt or kosher salt for sprinkling

4 tablespoons butter, melted

In a large bowl, combine the flours, malt powder, yeast, and salt, and stir to combine. In a separate bowl, stir together the oil, molasses, and hot water. Add this mixture to the flour mixture and stir to combine. When the dough comes together, turn it out onto a floured surface and knead until smooth and slightly tacky, about 10 minutes. Cover with a dish towel and allow to rest for 30 minutes.

Punch down the dough and turn it out onto a floured surface. Tear off a piece of the dough about the size of a lemon and roll it beneath the palms of your hands to form a 20-inch rope. This is best done on an unfloured surface with clean hands (you'll need a little stickiness to stretch the dough). If the dough shrinks from the length to which you stretched it, then roll it out as best you can and move on to the next. After you've rolled several, go back to the first one and work with it some more. Sometimes the dough takes a while to "remember" the shape you want it to take.

Preheat the oven to 400°F.

Shape the pretzels by first making a U facing away from you, then cross and twist the ends. Finally, fold them back toward you and pinch the ends where they meet the base to seal.

Fill a large bowl with the warm water and dissolve the baking soda in it. Holding the pretzels where the ends meet the base, dip the whole pretzel in the water for a few seconds, then blot the bottoms on a towel and arrange on a greased baking sheet. Sprinkle with the pretzel or kosher salt. Repeat with the remaining dough.

Bake for 12 to 15 minutes, or until golden. Brush with melted butter while they are still hot from the oven.

▶ *For hard-to-find baking ingredients, such as malt powder and pretzel salt, try The Baker's Catalogue at www.bakerscatalogue.com. Its companion sites, www.kingarthurflour.com and www.baking circle.com, are also great resources for learning to bake or expanding your baking repertoire.*

Five-Grain Bread

1 cup water

One 8-ounce cup plain
  yogurt

4 tablespoons butter or
  margarine

½ cup old fashioned or
  quick-cooking oats

⅓ cup wheat germ

⅓ cup unprocessed bran

4 to 4½ cups all purpose
  flour

1 cup whole wheat flour

¼ cup barley flour

½ cup packed brown sugar

Two ¼-ounce packages
  active dry yeast

2 teaspoons salt

1 large egg plus 1 egg lightly
  beaten

Wheat germ or oats for
  topping

In a medium saucepan over high heat, bring the water, yogurt, and butter to a boil. Stir in the oats, wheat germ, and bran. Remove from the heat and set aside until the mixture cools slightly but is still very warm (120° to 130°F).

In a large bowl, combine 1⅓ cups of all-purpose flour, the whole wheat flour, barley flour, sugar, yeast, and salt. Stir in the warm oats and bran mixture. Beat with an electric mixer on medium speed for 2 minutes, scraping the bowl occasionally. Add the egg and 1 cup of all-purpose flour, and beat for 2 minutes at high speed. Stir in enough of the remaining flour to make a soft dough. Knead on a lightly greased surface until smooth and elastic, about 8 to 10 minutes. Cover and let rest for 10 minutes.

Divide the dough in half and roll each half into a 12 × 7-inch rectangle. Beginning at the short end, roll it up tightly as you would for a jelly roll. Pinch the seams and ends to seal. Place the loaves, seam side down, in 2 greased 8½ × 4½-inch loaf pans. Cover and let rise in a warm draft-free place until doubled in size, about 1 hour.

Preheat the oven to 375°F.

With a sharp knife, make 3 diagonal slashes, ¼ inch deep, in each loaf. Brush with the beaten egg and sprinkle with the wheat germ. Bake for 40 minutes, or until golden brown on top. Remove the loaves from the pans and let cool on a wire rack.

▶ *Join your industry and trade association groups, and look for ways you can contribute before looking for things you can take away. As a contributor your stature and credibility increase, and before long your peers will be coming to you with opportunities.*

Focaccia Bread

MAKES 1 FOCACCIA LOAF

2¾ cups all purpose flour
One ¼ ounce package instant yeast
2½ teaspoons oregano
½ teaspoon salt
1 cup very warm water (120° to 130°F)
2 tablespoons olive oil
1 egg
Optional toppings (see below)

In a large bowl, combine 1½ cups of flour, the yeast, oregano, and salt. Stir the water and oil into the dry ingredients. Stir in the egg and enough of the remaining flour to make a soft dough. Cover and let rest for 10 minutes.

With lightly oiled hands, spread the dough in an oiled 9 × 13-inch pan. Spread with the selected topping. Cover loosely with plastic wrap and let rise in a warm, draft-free place until almost doubled in size, about 15 to 30 minutes.

Preheat the oven to 400°F.

Bake for 25 minutes, or until done. Let the bread cool in the pan on a wire rack or serve warm, cut into squares.

OPTIONAL TOPPINGS

ONION AND HERB: Combine ¼ cup of olive oil and 1½ cups of thinly sliced onion in a large skillet over medium heat and cook for 3 to 4 minutes, stirring occasionally, until the onions are soft but not browned. Spread the onion mixture over the dough. Sprinkle with 1 teaspoon of crushed rosemary and 1 teaspoon of coarse salt, if desired.

PARMESAN AND PECAN: Drizzle ¼ cup of olive oil over the dough. Sprinkle with ¾ cup of chopped pecans and ¼ cup of grated Parmesan cheese. Press the nuts into the dough.

BLUE CHEESE AND WALNUTS: Drizzle ¼ cup of olive oil over the dough. Sprinkle with ¾ cup of chopped walnuts and ½ cup of crumbled blue cheese. Press the nuts into the dough.

▶ *In most bread recipes that call for one packet of yeast, you can create a more aromatic and chewy texture by starting with a flourless sponge. To make a flourless sponge, dissolve one ¼-ounce package of active dry yeast in ½ cup of water and let the sponge sit overnight. The final rising might be shorter than called for in the recipe.*

Fresh Blueberry Banana Bread

MAKES 1 LOAF

1 cup fresh blueberries, washed and drained	½ teaspoon salt
1¾ cups all purpose flour	⅓ cup margarine
2 teaspoons baking powder	⅔ cup sugar
¼ teaspoon baking soda	2 eggs
	1 cup mashed ripe banana

Preheat the oven to 350°F.

Toss the blueberries with 2 tablespoons of flour. In a large bowl, sift together the rest of the flour, baking powder, baking soda, and salt. Set aside. In a separate bowl, cream the margarine and gradually beat in the sugar until fluffy. Beat in the eggs, 1 at a time. Add the flour mixture alternately with the mashed banana, stirring until blended. Stir in the blueberries. Bake in a greased 8½ × 4½-inch loaf pan for 50 to 60 minutes, or until a tester inserted in the middle comes out clean.

▶ *If the last banana in the bunch gets overly ripe, peel it and store in a plastic bag in the freezer until you have enough to make this recipe.*

Grandma Klusmeier's Strawberry Shortcake

MAKES 6 SERVINGS

Here's a local classic from Klusmeier's Restaurant, which was down the road from us in Linton, Indiana. The restaurant is gone now, but the flavors live on. —BETTE

1½ quarts fresh strawberries, sliced

2 cups sugar

2 cups self-rising flour

⅔ cup solid vegetable shortening

⅔ cup milk

¼ pound (1 stick) butter, melted

Whipped cream (optional)

Preheat the oven to 450°F.

In a large bowl, blend together the strawberries and sugar. Set aside. The berries and the juice will be the topping for the shortcake.

To make the shortcake: In a large bowl, sift the flour and then cut in the shortening until the particles are the size of rice. Add the milk all at once and mix it in lightly and quickly with a fork. When the dough begins to hold together, knead it lightly. Pat into 2 thin rounds about 8 inches across.

Bake the shortcakes on an ungreased 10 × 14-inch baking (biscuit) sheet (see Product List, page 253) until golden brown, 10 to 15 minutes. To serve, split the layers apart, put on a serving dish, and drizzle with the melted butter. Spoon the strawberries and juice generously on each layer and stack them. Serve warm with whipped cream, if desired.

▶ *In everything you do and in everything that happens, find a reason to give thanks.*

Garlicky Parmesan and Pepper Dinner Biscuits

MAKES 1 DOZEN BISCUITS

A prizewinning recipe from the 2003 Doughmakers Baking Contest, submitted by Alice Trimble, Terre Haute, Indiana.

2 cups all-purpose flour

1 tablespoon baking powder

2 teaspoons sugar

½ teaspoon cream of tartar

¼ teaspoon salt

¼ teaspoon baking soda

¼ teaspoon cracked black pepper

½ teaspoon garlic powder

¼ cup grated parmesan cheese

½ cup solid vegetable shortening

⅔ cup sour milk*

Preheat the oven to 450°F.

Combine the flour, baking powder, sugar, cream of tartar, salt, baking soda, pepper, garlic powder, and cheese in a medium bowl. Using a pastry knife, cut in the shortening until the mixture resembles coarse crumbs. Make a well in the center of the dry ingredients, pour in the milk, and stir with a fork until well moistened. Turn the dough out onto a floured surface and knead it for a few strokes, until nearly smooth. Pat it out to ¼ inch thick and cut circles with a biscuit cutter. Place the circles 1 inch apart on a 10 × 14-inch biscuit sheet (see Product List, page 253) and bake for 10 to 12 minutes. Serve warm with butter.

*To make sour milk, combine 1 tablespoon vinegar or lemon juice with 1 cup milk.

▶ *In all you do, conduct yourself honorably. An honest business woman's pillow is her peace of mind.*

Grandma B's Bread

MAKES 4 LOAVES

Sandy Brosnan of Terre Haute, Indiana, wanted to see her mother-in law's bread included because she says our pans are the only thing that could improve the results of this seventy-year-old family recipe.
—BETTE

1 cup powdered dry milk	Two ¼-ounce packages active
1 cup sugar	dry yeast
3 cups water	1 cup warm water
4 teaspoons salt	4 eggs
1 cup solid vegetable shortening	8 to 10 cups flour
2 cups quick oats	

Heat the milk, sugar, water, salt, and shortening in a large saucepan over medium heat until the shortening has melted. Remove from the heat, add the oats, and stir. Let the mixture sit for about 1 hour to cool to room temperature. In a small bowl, dissolve the yeast in the warm water and add to the oats mixture. Beat 1 egg and add it to the mixture, then repeat with the remaining eggs. Add the flour, 1 cup at a time, mixing after each addition, until the dough is too stiff to hand-mix. Turn the dough out on a floured surface and knead until it is soft and easy to handle, about 10 minutes.

Place the dough in a greased bowl and cover. Let it rise until double in size, about 2½ hours.

Preheat the oven to 370°F. Grease 4 8½ × 4½-inch loaf pans.

Punch the dough down and divide it into 4 pieces. Shape each piece into a loaf by rolling it into a ¼-inch rectangle and then rolling it up, starting with the short end. Place the loaves in the prepared pans. Cover and let rise for about 1½ hours.

Bake the loaves for 25 to 30 minutes. Allow them to cool before slicing.

▶ *If you store your flour in a functional widemouthed container instead of in a decorative canister, it will be much easier to scoop and measure.*

Pull-Apart Wheat Rolls

MAKES 2 DOZEN OR MORE

1 cup warm water (110° to 115°F)

One ¼-ounce package active dry yeast

1 teaspoon granulated sugar

¼ cup firmly packed brown sugar

¾ teaspoon salt

½ cup wheat germ

1 egg

3 tablespoons butter, softened

1½ cups whole wheat flour

1½ cups white flour

Place the warm water in a large bowl and stir in the yeast and granulated sugar. Let the mixture stand until the yeast starts to bubble. Add the brown sugar, salt, wheat germ, egg, butter, and whole wheat flour, and beat until smooth. Add the white flour, a little at a time, and stir with a wooden spoon until the dough becomes easy to handle.

Place the dough in a greased bowl, turning the dough to grease the top. Cover the bowl and let the dough rise in a warm, draft-free place until doubled in size, about 1½ hours.

Punch down the dough and with lightly greased hands pinch off some dough and form it into a ball about 1½ inches in diameter. Grease two 9-inch round cake pans and arrange the balls in the pan, leaving about ½ inch to ¾ inch between the balls so they have room to rise. Cover the pans and allow the balls to rise until they have doubled in size, about 45 minutes.

Preheat the oven to 375°F and bake the rolls about 20 to 25 minutes, or until the tops are brown.

▶ *Accept compliments graciously and give them generously.*

Grandma Ruth's Yeast Rolls

MAKES 45 TO 50

The search committee at our church called a new pastor in Texas. We really hoped he would come, so while we were waiting to hear his answer, I baked a batch of these rolls and sent them south. I included a note with the rolls that said to please accept them as a gesture of goodwill and as the blatant bribe they were meant to be! I trust that the Lord would have blessed our congregation with Reverend Watson and his family without my bread, but our new pastor did say it was the rolls that brought him to Terre Haute. —SANDRA ROBERTS, TERRE HAUTE, INDIANA

1 cup milk	1 cup warm water
½ cup sugar	Two ¼-ounce packages active dry yeast
1 tablespoon salt	3 eggs
6 tablespoons margarine	7 to 8 cups flour

In a medium saucepan over medium heat, heat the milk, sugar, salt, and margarine until the sugar dissolves, then cool to lukewarm. In a large mixing bowl, combine the water and yeast. Add the eggs and milk mixture, and beat. Add the flour, 1 cup at a time, until you have a workable dough.

Turn the dough out onto a work surface and knead with your hands until any loose bits of flour are mixed in. Return the dough to the bowl and cover it with plastic wrap. Let it rise in a warm place for about 1 hour, or until doubled in size.

Punch down the dough and then press or roll it out to ¾ inch thick. Cut out the rolls with a 2-inch biscuit cutter, then lay the back of a knife across the center and fold each roll in half to form a half-circle. Arrange the rolls on a lightly greased 13 × 18-inch sheet cake pan. If desired, brush the tops with melted butter or margarine. Cover with plastic wrap and let the rolls rise until doubled in size, about 1 hour.

Preheat the oven to 350°F. Bake the rolls for about 12 minutes, or until golden brown.

▶ *Don't rush through your recipes. Allow yourself time to really enjoy your baking. While you work, think about the friends and loved ones with whom you plan to share the freshly baked goodies.*

Orange Scones

2½ cups all purpose flour, plus additional for dusting

2 teaspoons baking powder

½ teaspoon salt

¼ pound (1 stick) cold butter, cut into pieces

½ cup sugar

¾ cup coarsely chopped dried cranberries

¾ cup half-and half

1 egg

1 tablespoon grated orange peel

ALMOND BUTTER:

¼ pound (1 stick) butter, softened

2 tablespoons confectioners' sugar

½ teaspoon almond extract

Preheat the oven to 375°F.

In a large bowl, combine the flour, baking powder, and salt. Cut the butter in with a pastry blender until the mixture resembles coarse crumbs. Add the sugar and cranberries, and stir until well combined.

In another bowl, stir together the half-and-half, egg, and orange peel until smooth. Add to the flour mixture and mix just until the flour is moistened. Turn the dough out onto a lightly floured surface and knead 8 to 10 times, until smooth. Add a small amount of flour if necessary.

Divide the dough in half and press each half into a 7-inch circle. Place the circles 2 inches apart on a large ungreased baking sheet. Score each half into 8 wedges but do not cut the wedges. Bake for 25 to 30 minutes, or until lightly browned. Cool on the baking sheet until warm.

Meanwhile, make the almond butter: Combine the butter, sugar, and almond extract in a small mixing bowl and beat at medium speed for 1 to 2 minutes, until well mixed. Scrape the bowl often during mixing.

Separate the scones while warm and serve with the almond butter. Store leftover scones in an airtight container at room temperature. Store the remaining almond butter, covered, in the refrigerator.

▶ *A pastry blender is made of 5 or 6 parallel U-shaped steel wires attached at both ends to a handle. It cuts the butter into small pieces so that the flour can coat the particles. Two knives may also be used.*

Home-Style Honey Wheat Bread

MAKES 3 LOAVES

A prizewinning recipe from the 2003 Doughmakers Baking Contest, submitted by Jan Darr, Terre Haute, Indiana.

3 cups warm water (110°F)

Two ¼-ounce packages active dry yeast

⅔ cup honey

5 cups white bread flour

5 tablespoons butter, melted

1 tablespoon salt

5 to 6 cups whole wheat flour

2 tablespoons cracked wheat

1 tablespoon vegetable oil

In a large bowl, mix the water, yeast, and ⅓ cup of honey. Add the white bread flour and stir to combine. Let set for 30 minutes, or until big and bubbly.

Mix in 3 tablespoons of melted butter, the remaining ⅓ cup of honey, and the salt. Stir in 2 cups of the whole wheat flour and the cracked wheat. Add up to 4 more cups of whole wheat flour, 1 cup at a time, mixing well after each addition. Add enough until the dough is tacky but can be worked with your hands. Flour a flat surface with the remaining whole wheat flour and knead the dough until it forms a smooth ball but is still sticky to touch. Grease a large bowl with vegetable oil. Place the dough in the bowl and turn it to coat the surface of the dough. Cover and let the dough rise until doubled in size, about 1 hour.

Punch the dough down and divide it into 3 loaves. Place them in greased 8½ × 4½-inch loaf pans and let rise until the dough is 1 inch above the rim of the loaf pans, about 1 hour.

Preheat the oven to 350°F and bake for 30 minutes. Remove the breads from the pans and brush them with the remaining 2 tablespoons of melted butter. Allow the loaves to cool about 30 minutes before slicing. The bread will keep in a sealed plastic bag for several days or may be frozen in a sealed plastic bag for a couple of weeks.

▶ *Answer the phone as if you are excited to receive every call.*

Ham and Dill Scones

MAKES 16 SCONES

These are great to pass at a cocktail party or reception where you want some substantial finger food.

2 cups all-purpose flour, plus
    additional for dusting
1 tablespoon baking powder
½ teaspoon baking soda
½ teaspoon salt
½ teaspoon dried dill weed
¼ pound (1 stick) cold butter
½ cup finely grated cheddar
    cheese

1 egg
⅓ cup apple juice
⅓ cup half-and half
3 tablespoons honey mustard
16 thin slices cheddar cheese,
    2 inches square
4 ounces thinly sliced
    deli ham

Preheat the oven to 400°F.

In a medium bowl, combine the flour, baking powder, baking soda, salt, and dill weed, and stir until well combined. Cut in the butter until the mixture resembles coarse crumbs. Add the grated cheese and stir until well mixed.

In a separate bowl, beat the egg into the apple juice and half-and half with a fork. Add this to the flour mixture and stir until just moistened. Turn the dough out onto a lightly floured surface and knead 10 times. With lightly floured hands, press the dough into two 9-inch circles that are about ½ inch thick.

Cut the dough with a floured 2-inch biscuit cutter or cookie cutter in the desired shape and place on a baking sheet. Bake for 10 to 15 minutes, or until lightly browned, then let cool on a wire rack.

To serve: Split the scones in half and spread each side with a little honey mustard. Add a thin slice of cheese and one slice of ham to each half. Alternatively, split each scone in half and spread the bottom half lightly with honey mustard. Layer with 1 half slice of cheese, 1 slice of ham, and another half slice of cheese, then place the top of the scone.

▶ *Find a way to stand behind your product or service in a visible and memorable way. We stamp our company name and phone number on the bottom of every pan we make. This often persuades a skeptic to give our pans a try because they see we believe in our product enough to do this.*

English Bath Buns

MAKES 2 DOZEN

½ cup warm water (100° to 110°F)

2 ¼-ounce packages active dry yeast

½ cup warm milk (100° to 110°F)

¼ pound (1 stick) butter or margarine, softened

2 tablespoons sugar

1 teaspoon salt

4 cups all-purpose flour, plus some additional for dusting

3 large eggs

2 teaspoons oil

¼ cup sugar

1 cup chopped almonds

Place the water in a large prewarmed bowl of an electric mixer. Sprinkle in the yeast and stir until dissolved. Add the milk, butter, sugar, salt, and 2 cups of flour. Beat for 2 minutes at medium speed. Add 2 eggs and another ½ cup of flour. Beat for 2 minutes at high speed, scraping the bowl occasionally. Stir in just enough of the remaining flour to make a soft dough. Turn the dough out onto a lightly floured surface and knead until smooth and elastic, about 10 minutes. Grease a large bowl with the oil. Place the dough in it and turn it to grease all sides. Cover with plastic wrap and let rise in a warm, draft-free place until doubled in size, about 1 hour.

Punch the dough down and turn out onto a lightly floured surface. Divide the dough into 24 equal pieces and shape each piece into a smooth ball. Grease 2 regular-size 12-cup muffin pans. Place a ball in each muffin cup. Cover with a clean kitchen towel and let rise in a warm, draft free place until doubled in size, about 30 minutes.

Preheat the oven to 375°F.

In a small bowl, whisk together the remaining egg with 1 tablespoon of water. Brush the tops of the buns with this egg mixture. Sprinkle the sugar and almonds over the top. Bake for 20 minutes, or until done. Remove the buns from the pans to cool on a wire rack.

▶ *Stir flour to loosen it before measuring. Always spoon flour into a measuring cup to overflowing and then level it with the back of a knife.*

Homemade Hamburger Buns

MAKES 2 TO 3 DOZEN DEPENDING ON SIZE

Once you've had a sandwich on a homemade bun, it's hard to go back to those store boughts!
—JOYCE MCCLELLAND, DOUGHMAKERS' FIRST EMPLOYEE AND LEAD CUSTOMER SERVICE REPRESENTATIVE.

½ cup plus 1 tablespoon sugar	One ¼-ounce package active dry yeast
1 teaspoon salt	¼ cup warm water
¼ cup solid vegetable shortening	2 eggs, beaten
2 cups milk, scalded	6½ to 7 cups flour

Place ½ cup of sugar, salt, and shortening in a large bowl. Pour the scalded milk over and stir until dissolved. Allow the mixture to cool until lukewarm (90° to 100°F), about 5 minutes. Dissolve the yeast in the warm water with the 1 tablespoon of sugar, then add the yeast mixture to the milk mixture and blend. Add the eggs and beat well. Stir in 4 cups of flour and beat well. Add 2½ to 3 more cups of flour to make a stiff dough. Knead for 5 to 10 minutes by hand or for 3 to 4 minutes in a stand mixer.

Roll the dough out to ½ to ¾ inch thick and cut it into circles of 3 to 4 inches in diameter or to desired size. Place the circles on ungreased baking sheets. Cover the buns with a damp tea towel or plastic wrap and let rise for 2 to 2½ hours.

Preheat the oven to 375°F. Bake the buns for 10 to 12 minutes, until the tops are golden brown. Allow the buns to cool on a wire rack. Use them right away or store them in zippered plastic bags in the freezer for up to 1 month.

▶ *Because 3- to 4-inch biscuit cutters are hard to come by, clean and save the lid from a 28-ounce can of tomatoes or peaches. Use it for cutting out these buns.*

Raisin Pumpkin Bread

MAKES 1 LOAF

1 cup granulated sugar

1 cup canned pumpkin

2 eggs

½ cup firmly packed brown sugar

½ cup oil

2 cups sifted all-purpose flour

1 teaspoon baking soda

½ teaspoon salt

½ teaspoon cinnamon

½ teaspoon nutmeg

¼ teaspoon ginger

½ teaspoon baking powder

1 cup raisins

½ cup toasted walnuts, chopped

¼ cup water

Preheat the oven to 350°F. Grease an 8½ × 4½-inch loaf pan.

In a large mixing bowl, combine the granulated sugar, pumpkin, eggs, brown sugar, and oil. Beat with an electric mixer until well blended. In another bowl, sift together the flour, baking soda, salt, cinnamon, nutmeg, ginger, and baking powder. Combine this with the pumpkin mixture, mixing well. Fold in the raisins, nuts, and water. Turn the batter into the prepared loaf pan. Bake for 65 to 75 minutes, or until a tester inserted in the middle comes out clean. Cool the bread in the pan for 5 minutes, then turn it out onto a wire rack to cool thoroughly.

▶ *A Danish dough whisk looks like a small rug beater, but once you use one, you may consider it your secret weapon in baking success. It is just the thing for mixing wet, gloppy dough. Ask for it in your kitchen supply store.*

Sweet Rolls

MAKES 35 ROLLS

DOUGH:

Three ¼-ounce packages dry yeast

¾ cup plus 1 teaspoon sugar

¾ cup warm water

3 cups milk, scalded (see Tip)

3 teaspoons salt

¾ cup margarine

3 eggs, beaten

12 cups all-purpose flour

FILLING:

8 ounces raisins

¾ to 1 pound brown sugar, depending on taste

1 cup granulated sugar

4 teaspoons cinnamon

One pound (4 sticks) butter, melted

1 cup chopped pecans

GLAZE:

4 ounces cream cheese

¼ pound (1 stick) butter, softened

2 cups confectioners' sugar (approximately)

1 to 2 tablespoons milk, if needed

To make the dough: Dissolve the yeast and 1 teaspoon of sugar in the warm water. Add the scalded milk and stir in the remaining sugar and the salt. Add the margarine and stir until dissolved. Allow the mixture to cool.

Combine the yeast mixture, eggs, and milk mixture, and pour into the large bowl of a mixer fitted with a dough hook. Add the flour, 2 cups at a time, and mix at medium-slow speed after each addition. When all the flour has been used, mix on medium speed for 3 to 4 minutes. Transfer the dough to an oiled bowl and cover with plastic wrap. Let it rise until doubled in size, about 1 hour.

To make the filling: Cover the raisins with warm water for 10 minutes or more, then drain. Mix together the brown sugar, granulated sugar, and cinnamon.

Divide the dough in half and roll one half into a rectangle, approximately 8 × 16 inches. Brush with half of the melted butter, then sprinkle with half of the sugar and cinnamon mixture. Press the sugar mixture down with your fingertips. Sprinkle half of the raisins and pecans over the top. Roll the dough lengthwise as if for a jelly roll. Seal the seam and cut into 1-inch slices. Brush again with the melted butter. Place the slices flat in a greased 13 × 18-inch sheet cake pan. Repeat with the remaining dough and ingredients. Let rise until double in size, about 1 hour.

Preheat the oven to 400°F. Bake for 12 to 15 minutes.

While baking the rolls, prepare the glaze: Mix the cream cheese, butter, and sugar together. Thin the glaze with 1 to 2 tablespoons of milk, if necessary, so the glaze will spread easily. Spread the glaze on the rolls while they are still warm and serve immediately

▶ *To scald milk, heat it in a heavy-bottomed saucepan over medium heat, stirring occasionally. As soon as bubbles form around the inside edges of the pan, remove it from the heat.*

Swiss Cheese Bread

MAKES 2 LOAVES

1 cup milk

2 tablespoons sugar

1 tablespoon salt

1 tablespoon butter

One ¼-ounce package active
dry yeast

1 cup warm water

5 cups all-purpose flour
(approximately)

8 ounces Swiss cheese, grated

In a medium saucepan over medium-high heat, scald the milk with the sugar, salt, and butter. Let cool until lukewarm. Dissolve the yeast in the warm water, then stir in the warm milk mixture. Beat in 2 cups of flour, the cheese, and the remaining flour, about 3 cups, to make a stiff dough. Knead until smooth and elastic, 8 to 10 minutes. Use only enough flour to keep the dough from sticking.

Place the dough into a large greased bowl and turn to coat the dough. Let rise for 1½ to 2 hours, or until double in size. Punch down, divide the dough in half, and knead each half a few times. Shape into 2 loaves and place them in 2 greased 8½ × 4½-inch loaf pans. Cover and let rise in a warm place for 30 minutes to 1 hour, until the dough rises about ½ inch above the pan.

Preheat the oven to 350°F and bake for about 50 minutes.

Remove the loaves from the pans and let cool on wire racks. Wrapped tightly, these breads freeze well for up to 2 weeks, and they're delicious at breakfast when toasted and buttered.

▶ *Listen to your customers and do everything you can to meet their requests. They might forgive you for saying "no," but they'll remember you for saying "yes."*

Breakfast Breads

Apple Bread Pudding

MAKES 8 TO 10 SERVINGS

5 slices firm white bread

Zest of 1 medium lemon,
  finely chopped

⅓ cup granulated sugar

3 medium Yellow Delicious
  apples

¼ teaspoon freshly grated
  nutmeg, plus extra for
  sprinkling

4 large eggs

2 teaspoons vanilla extract

1½ cups heavy cream

Confectioners' sugar

Preheat the oven to 350°F. Generously butter the bottom and sides of a 9-inch square cake pan.

Tear the bread slices into quarters. Chop them medium-fine with the metal blade of a food processor until they yield about 1⅓ cups of crumbs. Transfer to a small bowl.

In a medium bowl, stir the lemon zest into the granulated sugar. Core and peel the apples, then slice them thinly into rings.

To assemble the pudding: Sprinkle 2 tablespoons of bread crumbs on the bottom of the prepared pan. Layer ⅓ of the apple slices on the crumbs and sprinkle with ⅓ of the lemon-sugar mixture, a little nutmeg, and 2 more tablespoons of bread crumbs. Repeat the layering twice more and use the remaining crumbs to make a thick layer on top.

Combine the eggs and vanilla in a food processor fitted with a metal blade and beat well. Pour in 1 cup of the cream and continue beating. Pour the egg-cream mixture slowly over the apples, letting it seep through the layers. Bake in the center of the oven for 30 minutes, then lower the temperature to 300°F and continue baking until the apples are tender, about 15 minutes more. Cool the pudding in the baking dish set on a wire rack. Sprinkle with confectioners' sugar and serve slightly warm or at room temperature.

Just before serving, whip the remaining ½ cup of cream and serve it in a separate bowl sprinkled with nutmeg.

▶ *Narrow your focus and then focus your brand. We've been asked countless times if we are going to make cookware. The answer is always no. The cookware market might be fifteen times larger than the bakeware market, but there is easily thirty times more competition. By focusing all our branding efforts on bakeware, we create a stronger impact for our brand: Doughmakers is bakeware.*

Peach Bread

MAKES 6 SERVINGS

One 29-ounce can peach halves or slices, drained
5 slices bread, with crust trimmed
1½ cups sugar
2 tablespoons flour
1 egg
¼ pound (1 stick) butter, melted

Preheat the oven to 350°F.

Slice the peach halves into thirds and spread them in the bottom of a 9-inch square pan. Cut the bread into strips and layer them over the peaches. In a medium bowl, combine the sugar, flour, egg, and butter, and pour over the peaches and bread.

Bake for about 20 minutes, until bubbly and golden brown. Spoon into bowls.

▶ *Clean your Doughmakers Bakeware with a good grease-fighting detergent such as Dawn and hot water. You can let it soak for 15 minutes or so if necessary. A pan is easier to clean right after you use it than after it has been left in the sink for a few hours or days.*

Apple Harvest Danish

Every time I make this dish, I think of Kelley's Apple Farm near Rochester, New York, where we used to pick apples when we were growing up. Simple memories like that one, brought to life by simple recipes like this one, is reason enough to keep the tradition of baking alive. —BETTE

4 eggs
¾ cup sugar
1 cup heavy cream
2½ cups milk
¼ pound (1 stick) butter, melted
1 tablespoon vanilla extract
1 teaspoon cinnamon
8 ounces cream cheese
1 baguette, cut into ¼ inch slices

5 Granny Smith apples, peeled and thinly sliced
½ cup golden raisins

CRUMB TOPPING:
1 cup flour
½ cup brown sugar
1 teaspoon cinnamon
¼ pound (1 stick) cold butter

Whisk together the eggs, sugar, cream, milk, butter, vanilla, and cinnamon. Spread a little cream cheese on each slice of bread.

Grease a 9 × 13-inch pan with butter. Use ⅓ of the apples to make a layer in the bottom of the pan. Sprinkle with ⅓ of the raisins and follow with a layer of the bread slices. Repeat. Place the remaining apples and another ⅓ of the raisins on top of the bread. Pour the egg mixture over the top.

Preheat the oven to 350°

To make the crumb topping: Place the flour, sugar, and cinnamon in a bowl. Cut the cold butter into the mixture until you get the desired crumbly topping texture. Add the remaining raisins. Sprinkle the topping evenly over the bread and egg mixture. Bake for 45 to 50 minutes, until the top is lightly browned

▶ *Beware of expensive turnkey solutions to the problems you face in your business. There really is no substitute for doing the hard work of building your company.*

Apricot Almond Delights

MAKES ABOUT 4 DOZEN

A prizewinning recipe from the 2003 Doughmakers Baking Contest, submitted by Rae Ann Webster of Terre Haute, Indiana.

DOUGH:

One ¼-ounce package active dry yeast

1½ cups warm water

1 cup plus 1 teaspoon sugar

1 cup solid vegetable shortening or ⅔ cup butter or margarine and ⅓ cup solid vegetable shortening

1½ teaspoons salt

3 eggs

1 cup lukewarm mashed potatoes

1 tablespoon vanilla extract

7 to 7½ cups unbleached flour or bread flour

FILLING:

¼ pound (1 stick) butter, melted

8 tablespoons cinnamon

1 cup sugar

2 cups finely chopped dried apricots

2 cups sliced almonds

FROSTING:

2 tablespoons butter, softened

2½ cups confectioners' sugar

2 tablespoons apricot preserves

2 tablespoons milk

1 tablespoon almond flavoring

GARNISH (OPTIONAL):

1 cup chopped dried apricots

1 cup sliced almonds

Dissolve the yeast in the water. Add 1 teaspoon of sugar and mix to dissolve. Set aside.

In a large bowl, cream the shortening and 1 cup of sugar. Add the salt, eggs, mashed potatoes, and vanilla. Add the yeast mixture and 4 cups of flour, and beat until smooth. Mix in the remaining flour until the dough is easy to handle. Turn out onto a lightly floured board and knead until smooth and elastic, about 5 minutes. Place the dough in a greased bowl and turn to coat. Cover tightly and refrigerate for at least 8 hours. The dough can be kept in the refrigerator up to 7 days.

Punch down the dough and divide it into 4 equal pieces. Roll 1 piece of dough on a lightly floured board into a rectangular shape, approximately 9 × 13 × 1 inch thick. Coat the top with melted butter. Mix the cinnamon and sugar together and sprinkle ¼ of the mixture over the butter. Sprinkle with ½ cup of chopped apricots and ½ cup of sliced almonds. Starting on the long side, roll the dough as you would a jelly roll and seal the seam by pinching the dough together. Cut the roll into 1-inch-thick slices and place them on an ungreased baking sheet. Brush the tops with melted butter, cover with waxed paper, and allow to rise until one-third larger in size, about 30 minutes.

Repeat the process with the remaining dough pieces. The dough keeps well in the refrigerator, so one-fourth of it can be used at a time to allow for fresh rolls in 4 smaller batches (family size), or it can be baked all at once for larger groups.

When you are ready to bake, preheat the oven to 375°F. Bake the rolls for 18 to 20 minutes, until lightly browned. Watch closely and do not overbake them. Remove the rolls from the baking sheet and allow to cool on wire racks for 5 to 8 minutes.

Mix all the frosting ingredients together and spread on the rolls. Sprinkle with additional almonds and chopped apricots if desired. The rolls may be served warm or completely cooled. Place them in an airtight container for storage.

▶ *A good hand washing should be the first step in every recipe.*

Bev's Favorite Coffee Cake

MAKES 6 TO 8 SERVINGS

I always add fruit to this—whatever is in season or whatever I can get my hands on. I gently fold it into the batter as the last ingredients. About 1½ cups of fruit is needed. You may need to increase the time depending on the fruit. I usually check it at 40 to 45 minutes and continue cooking until the cake springs back when touched in the center. —Bev Bensky, Bette's and Diane's sister

2¼ cups flour

½ teaspoon salt

2 teaspoons cinnamon

¼ teaspoon ground ginger

1 cup brown sugar

¾ cup granulated sugar

¾ cup corn oil

1 cup chopped walnuts or pecans

1 teaspoon baking soda

1 teaspoon baking powder

1 egg, beaten

1 cup buttermilk

Preheat the oven to 350°F.

In a large bowl, mix together the flour, salt, 1 teaspoon of cinnamon, ginger, both sugars, and corn oil. Remove ¾ cup of this mixture and add to it the nuts with the remaining teaspoon of cinnamon. Mix well and set aside.

Add the baking soda, baking powder, egg, and buttermilk to the remaining batter and mix well. Small lumps in the batter are okay. Pour the batter into a well-greased 9 × 13-inch pan. Sprinkle the topping mixture evenly over the surface. Bake for 40 to 45 minutes, or until the cake springs back when touched in the center.

▶ *If you don't have buttermilk on hand, you can stir together 2¼ cups of milk and ¼ cup of vinegar to make 2½ cups of buttermilk.*

Blueberry Muffin Cake

2 cups all-purpose flour

1 cup sugar

2½ teaspoons baking powder

¾ teaspoon salt

2 cups blueberries

¾ cup milk

2 large eggs

4 tablespoons butter, melted

1 teaspoon vanilla extract

TOPPING:

⅓ cup all purpose flour

⅓ cup sugar

3 tablespoons butter, softened

½ teaspoon cinnamon

Preheat the oven to 350° F. Grease a 9-inch square cake pan.

In a large bowl, combine the flour, sugar, baking powder, and salt. Stir well with a fork and add the blueberries. Toss well to coat the berries with flour.

In a medium bowl, stir together the milk, eggs, butter, and vanilla. Add this to the dry ingredients and stir together until just blended. Spread the mixture in the prepared pan.

In a small bowl, blend the topping ingredients together with your fingers until crumbly. Sprinkle it over the batter. Bake the cake in the middle of the oven for 35 to 40 minutes, or until a cake tester comes out clean. Let the cake cool before cutting it into 3-inch squares. Serve with fresh fruit.

▸ *Keep your eyes on the prize, but enjoy the journey.*

Caramel Pecan Rolls

MAKES 2 DOZEN

A prizewinning recipe from the 2003 Doughmakers Baking Contest, submitted by Jan Darr, Terre Haute, Indiana.

2 cups milk
½ cup water
½ cup sugar
⅓ cup cornmeal
¼ pound (1 stick) butter or margarine
2 teaspoons salt
7 to 7½ cups unbleached flour
2½ tablespoons active dry yeast
¼ cup instant potato flakes
2 eggs

TOPPING:
2 cups brown sugar
¼ pound (1 stick) butter or margarine
½ cup milk
1 cup chopped pecans

FILLING:
¼ pound (1 stick) butter or
    margarine, at room temperature
½ cup sugar
2 teaspoons cinnamon

Combine the milk, water, sugar, cornmeal, butter, and salt in a medium saucepan and bring to a boil over medium-high heat. Remove from the heat and stir occasionally while cooling to lukewarm.

In a large bowl, combine 2 cups of flour, the yeast, and potato flakes. Add the lukewarm corn-meal mixture and stir well. Add the eggs and mix well. Stir in the remaining 3½ cups flour at this stage and mix with a wooden spoon.

Place the dough on a well-floured surface and knead until flour is incorporated and dough is smooth. Place in a large greased bowl and let rise until doubled in size, about 1 hour.

When the dough has doubled, prepare the topping: In a medium saucepan over medium heat, combine the brown sugar, butter, and milk. Bring to a boil, stirring occasionally. Pour evenly into 2 greased 9 × 13-inch pans or four 9-inch round pans. Sprinkle the pecans over the sugar mixture.

Prepare the filling: Mix the butter, sugar, and cinnamon well in a medium bowl. Punch down the dough and divide it in half. Roll each half into a 12 × 15-inch rectangle. Spread the filling to the edges of the rectangle. Roll up each rectangle, starting with the longer side, and cut it into 12 one-inch slices. Place the slices on the topping in the pans. Let rise until doubled, about 1 hour.

Heat the oven to 375°F and bake for 20 to 23 minutes, until golden brown. Invert the pans onto foil-lined baking sheets and allow to cool slightly before serving.

▶ *Be enthusiastic about your business; and other people will get caught up in the excitement!*

Cranberry Apple French Toast Bake

MAKES 9 TO 12 SERVINGS

This is an easy treat for breakfast when you have guests in the house because most of the recipe is made the night before. In the morning you can just pop it in the oven as the guests are waking up. —BETTE

4 eggs

¾ cup sugar

2½ cups milk

1 cup light cream

¼ pound (1 stick) butter, melted

1 tablespoon vanilla extract

1 teaspoon allspice

1 unpeeled apple, preferably Granny Smith, finely chopped or grated (a food processor works well for this)

1 cup finely chopped cranberries

½ cup raisins

1 baguette, approximately 2 inches in diameter, cut into about sixteen ¾- to 1-inch slices

Combine the eggs, sugar, milk, cream, butter, vanilla, and allspice in a medium bowl and mix well. In a large bowl, stir together the apple, cranberries, and raisins. Grease a 9 × 13-inch pan and pour ⅓ of the batter into the pan. Sprinkle about half or slightly more of the fruits over the batter.

Arrange the slices of bread in the pan and pour the remaining batter evenly over the bread. Sprinkle the remaining fruit on top. Let stand for 20 minutes or overnight in the refrigerator, covered with plastic.

Preheat the oven to 350°F and bake until the mixture has set and the top is lightly browned, about 50 minutes. Serve immediately.

▶ *Advertising can be effective, but it is expensive. On the other hand, editorial exposure is priceless. Work every angle to get newspapers, magazines, and TV and radio programs to tell your product's story for you.*

Apple Kolaches

MAKES 2 DOZEN

Kolaches, a Czech wedding pastry, are little pillows of dough with a filling in the center. Sometimes, as with this recipe, the corners of the dough are pulled up to partially enclose the filling. In our travels through Texas, customers have told us about the Caldwell Kolache Festival held each September. If you are down that way, drop by and say that you like to make your kolaches on Doughmakers bakeware!

2 cups sifted flour
½ pound (2 sticks) butter, softened
Two 3-ounce packages Philadelphia cream cheese, softened

2 or 3 Red Delicious apples, cored and finely chopped
Cinnamon to taste
2 cups confectioners' sugar
2 to 3 tablespoons water or milk
½ teaspoon vanilla extract

Sift the flour into a mixing bowl and add the butter and cream cheese. Work these ingredients together with your hands until the dough begins to form. Shape the dough into a ball, cover with plastic wrap, and refrigerate for several hours or overnight.

Preheat the oven to 400°F.

In a large bowl, toss the chopped apples with the cinnamon.

Roll out the dough to ¼ inch thick and cut it into 3½-inch squares. Place a heaping teaspoon of the apple mixture in the center of each square. Fold the four corners to the center over the filling and pinch the seams together to form a square. Place on an ungreased baking sheet and bake for 20 minutes, or until golden. Remove from the oven and cool slightly.

Make the glaze by mixing together the sugar, water, and vanilla in a medium bowl. Dribble the thick glaze over the warm kolaches.

▶ *Ask the locals for the best places to eat.*

Maple Oat Scones

MAKES 12 SERVINGS

2¼ cups all purpose flour

¼ cup sugar

1 tablespoon baking powder

⅔ cup quick cooking oats

12 tablespoons (1½ sticks) butter, well chilled and cut into small bits

¾ cup heavy cream

1 teaspoon vanilla extract

6 tablespoons pure maple syrup, plus 1 to 2 tablespoons for brushing

½ cup golden raisins

Preheat the oven to 400°F.

In a food processor, pulse together the flour, sugar, baking powder, and oats until well mixed. Add the butter and pulse until the mixture resembles coarse meal. Pour in the cream and vanilla, and pulse until just combined. Add 6 tablespoons of syrup and pulse again until blended. Fold in the raisins.

Turn the dough out onto a floured work surface. Gently pat out the dough and fold it back over itself about a half-dozen times, until smooth. (A dough scraper helps with this.) Use a light hand and don't overmix.

Divide the dough in half and pat it out again into two ¾-inch-thick disks. Score each disk into 6 plump pie-shaped wedges. Transfer the disks to a small, ungreased baking sheet and brush the sides and top with the remaining syrup.

Bake for 15 to 17 minutes, until light brown. Serve warm or at room temperature.

▶ *When life hands you lemons, make lemonade! It is a well-known saying but still one of our favorites. One time we meant to order ninety biscuit cutters for our shows and received 90 dozen. So what did we do? We gave a set of cutters to everyone who bought our biscuit sheet. The deal was so popular that we had to order more!*

Overnight Cinnamon Rolls

MAKES 32 ROLLS

One 18-ounce package
    French vanilla cake mix
5¼ cups all purpose flour
Two ¼-ounce packages active
    dry yeast
1 teaspoon salt
2½ cups warm water
½ cup sugar

2 teaspoons cinnamon
½ cup butter, melted
½ cup raisins
¾ cup chopped pecans
1 cup confectioners' sugar
3 tablespoons milk
½ teaspoon vanilla extract

Stir together the cake mix, flour, yeast, salt, and water in a large bowl. Cover with plastic wrap and let rise for about 1 hour, until doubled in size. Combine the sugar and cinnamon, and set aside until the dough is ready.

Turn the dough out onto a floured work surface and divide it in half. Roll one half into a rectangle, about 12 × 18 inches. Brush with half of the melted butter, sprinkle with half of the sugar-cinnamon mix, half of the raisins, and ¼ cup of pecans.

Starting with the long edge, roll the rectangle of dough into a log, sealing the seam with a wet finger. Cut the log into about sixteen 1-inch-thick slices. Place the slices in a lightly greased 9 × 13-inch pan. Repeat this process with the remaining dough and ingredients, reserving ¼ cup of pecans. Cover the pan with plastic wrap and let rise in the refrigerator overnight.

In the morning, remove from the refrigerator and let stand about 30 minutes. Preheat the oven to 350°F and bake the rolls for 25 minutes, or until the tops are golden brown. Allow to cool slightly.

Stir together the confectioners' sugar, milk, and vanilla. Drizzle over the rolls and sprinkle them with the remaining ¼ cup of pecans.

▶ *Nuts always benefit from toasting before use in a recipe because it brings out their flavor. Place the nuts on a jelly roll pan and toast them in a 350°F oven for 7 to 12 minutes. They are done when they are fragrant and slightly darker in color.*

Raspberry Apple Coffee Cake

MAKES 12 TO 15 SERVINGS

SAUCE:

3½ cups raspberries

1 cup water

2 tablespoons lemon juice

1½ cups sugar

⅓ cup cornstarch

BATTER:

1 large Granny Smith apple

3 cups all-purpose flour

1 cup sugar

1 teaspoon baking powder

1 teaspoon baking soda

½ pound (2 sticks) cold butter

2 eggs, beaten

1 cup sour cream

1 teaspoon vanilla extract

TOPPING:

½ cup flour

½ cup sugar

½ cup pecans, chopped

4 tablespoons cold butter

GLAZE:

¾ cup confectioners' sugar

3 ounces cream cheese, softened

½ teaspoon vanilla extract

3 tablespoons milk

Preheat the oven to 350°F.

Combine the raspberries and water in a saucepan over medium heat for 5 minutes, stirring occasionally. Remove from the heat and stir in the lemon juice, sugar, and cornstarch. Return to the heat and bring to a boil over medium-high heat. Stir until the mixture thickens, about 3 to 4 minutes. Set aside to cool to room temperature.

Peel and thinly slice the apple. In a large bowl, combine the flour, sugar, baking powder, and baking soda. Cut the butter into the flour mixture until the mixture is crumbly. Mix in the eggs, sour cream, and vanilla. The batter will be stiff.

Spoon half of the batter into the bottom of a 9 × 13-inch pan. Pour the raspberry sauce over the batter. Use a teaspoon to dollop half of the remaining batter over the sauce. Top with a layer of apples, using half of the slices. Follow with the rest of the batter and the remaining apples slices.

To make the topping: Mix the flour, sugar, and pecans, and cut in the butter. Sprinkle over the apples. Bake for 38 to 45 minutes, or until the coffee cake is set and the top has browned.

To make the glaze: Combine the confectioners' sugar, cream cheese, and vanilla. Stir in enough milk so the glaze is a good consistency for drizzling over the warm coffee cake.

▶ *The only benefit to imitation vanilla is for people who have an intolerance to alcohol. If that isn't a problem for you, always buy real vanilla extract, the best you can find.*

Cakes

Almond Polenta Cake with Lemon Syrup

MAKES 8 SERVINGS

Leslie Glover Pendleton, author of One Dough Fifty Cookies, *created this recipe for our friends down the street at Clabber Girl Baking Powder. When we launched our retail line of bakeware, Leslie was our spokesperson to the gourmet community and introduced us to the International Association of Culinary Professionals, whose members have been very supportive and encouraging.* —Bette

¾ cup olive oil
1½ cups sugar
1¼ cups yellow cornmeal
1 cup almonds
3 large eggs
1 egg yolk
1 teaspoon almond extract
1 cup milk
1 cup all-purpose flour
1½ teaspoons baking powder
1 teaspoon salt

SYRUP:
½ cup freshly squeezed lemon juice
½ cup sugar
2 tablespoons grappa or dry
    vermouth

CREAM:
8 ounces mascarpone cheese
⅓ cup sugar
½ teaspoon vanilla extract
1 cup heavy cream

Preheat the oven to 325° F. Butter and flour one 9-inch round cake pan.

Finely grind the almonds in a food processor. Using an electric mixer, beat together the oil, sugar, cornmeal, and almonds in a medium bowl. Add the eggs and yolk, and beat on high speed for 2 minutes, until lightened. Stir the almond extract into the milk in one bowl. In another bowl, stir together the flour, baking powder, and salt. Beat half of the milk into the cornmeal mixture, then beat in half of the flour. Beat in the rest of the milk and then the rest of the flour. Beat the batter for 1 additional minute and pour it into the prepared pan.

Bake the cake on the middle rack for 1 hour 10 minutes, or until a skewer inserted in the center comes out clean. Invert the cake onto a plate and invert it again onto a rack. While the cake is still warm, poke holes all over the top of it with a wooden skewer. Stir the syrup ingredients together in a bowl and brush the mixture all over the warm cake. Let cool.

With the whisk attachment beat the mascarpone with the sugar and vanilla until smooth. Add the cream and beat until it holds soft peaks. Serve with slices of the cake.

▶ *Tony Robbins put this inscription in one of his books: "Most people overestimate what they can do in a year, and underestimate what they can do in a decade." Stay focused on your goal!*

Black-and-White Roulade

MAKES TEN 1-INCH-THICK SLICES

CAKE:

¾ cup all purpose flour

¼ cup unsweetened cocoa

⅛ teaspoon salt

4 eggs

1 teaspoon instant espresso powder
or ground instant coffee

⅔ cup sugar

3 tablespoons butter, melted and
cooled

Confectioners' sugar

FILLING:

1¼ cups heavy cream

2 tablespoons confectioners' sugar

⅛ teaspoon cinnamon

SAUCE:

⅓ cup water

Four 1-ounce squares semisweet
baking chocolate, chopped

2 tablespoons unsalted butter

½ teaspoon instant espresso powder

⅛ teaspoon cinnamon

Heat the oven to 375° F. Grease a 10 × 15-inch jelly roll pan and line it with parchment paper. Grease and flour the parchment paper.

Combine the flour, cocoa, and salt in a medium bowl. Set aside. Beat the eggs in a large mixing bowl at medium-high speed until well mixed, about 1 to 2 minutes. Continue beating while adding the espresso powder, then gradually add the sugar until the mixture is thick and lemon-colored, about 5 minutes. Gently stir the flour-cocoa mixture into the egg mixture, ⅓ at a time. Beat just until combined after each addition.

Remove 1 cup of the batter and stir it with the melted butter in a small bowl. Working quickly, stir this mixture back into the rest of the batter. Spread the batter in the prepared pan.

Bake for 9 to 12 minutes, or until the center springs back lightly when touched with your finger. Immediately loosen the cake from the edges of the pan with a knife. Drape a clean kitchen towel sprinkled with confectioners' sugar over the pan and then invert it and the cake onto the towel. Remove the pan and peel off the parchment paper. While the cake is still hot, roll up the cake in the towel, starting with the 10-inch side. The towel will be wrapped inside the cake where the filling will go. Cool the cake completely and trim the edges slightly if crisp.

To make the filling: In a medium bowl using an electric hand mixer, beat the cream at medium speed until stiff peaks form, about 2 to 3 minutes. Set the mixer at a lower setting and add the sugar and cinnamon.

To assemble the roulade: Unroll the cooled cake and remove the towel. Spread the filling on the surface of the cake, leaving a ½-inch border all around. Starting at the short end, gently roll up the cake. Transfer to a serving platter, cover, and refrigerate until ready to serve.

To make the sauce: Combine the water, chocolate, butter, espresso powder, and cinnamon in a 1-quart saucepan. Cook over low heat, stirring constantly, until the chocolate has melted, 2 to 4 minutes.

To serve, cut the roulade into slices. Spoon the sauce on a dessert plate. (Alternatively, you can transfer the warm sauce to a pastry bag or a squeeze bottle with a narrow tip and decorate a broad-rimmed white plate.) Top with the roulade slice.

▶ *The secret to perfectly whipped cream: Start with cold heavy cream and chill the bowl and beaters if possible. Start whipping slowly, then gradually add speed. Stop beating when soft, floppy peaks form or when you can drop a dollop from a spoon. If you whip it too much, you'll have butter.*

Carrot Pineapple Cake

MAKES 15 SERVINGS

A prizewinning recipe from the 2003 Doughmakers Baking Contest, submitted by Pat Fisher, Terre Haute, Indiana.

CAKE:

2 cups all-purpose flour

2 cups sugar

2 teaspoons baking soda

2 teaspoons cinnamon

1 teaspoon salt

1½ cups vegetable oil

4 eggs or 1 cup egg substitute

Two 6-ounce jars carrot baby food

1 cup drained crushed pineapple

FROSTING:

One 8-ounce package cream cheese, softened to room temperature

¼ pound (1 stick) butter, softened to room temperature

1 teaspoon vanilla extract

1 to 2 tablespoons rum

4 cups confectioners' sugar

1 cup coarsely chopped walnuts

Preheat the oven to 350° F. Grease and flour two 9-inch round baking pans or one deep pan (see Tip below for cutting into layers).

In the large mixing bowl of a stand mixer, combine the flour, sugar, baking soda, cinnamon, and salt. Add the oil, eggs, and baby food, and mix on low speed until well blended. Stir in the pineapple. Pour the mixture into the prepared pan or pans. Bake for 35 to 40 minutes, or until a toothpick inserted in the center comes out clean. Cool the layers for 10 minutes, then remove from the pans and place on wire racks to cool completely.

In a large mixing bowl, beat together the cream cheese and butter until very smooth. Beat in the vanilla and rum. While continuing to beat the frosting, slowly add the confectioners' sugar. Beat until the mixture reaches a good spreading consistency.

Place 1 layer on a serving plate. Spread frosting on top, then add the second layer. Frost the top and sides of the cake and sprinkle the nuts on top. Refrigerate up to 1 day before serving.

▶ *To slice a cake into layers: Wrap the circumference with unflavored dental floss and cross the ends. Make sure the floss is centered all the way around the cake. Pull out on the ends to tighten the floss around the cake and pull the floss through the center of the cake.*

Chocolate Zucchini Cake

MAKES ABOUT 20 SERVINGS

This recipe is adapted for our pans by Annie Watts, from a recipe she contributed to Picnic, Potlucks & Prizewinners: Celebrating Indiana Hospitality with 4-H Families and Friends, *Indianapolis, Indiana.*

CAKE:

3 cups all-purpose flour

1½ teaspoons Clabber Girl baking powder

1 teaspoon baking soda

1 teaspoon cinnamon

½ teaspoon salt

1 cup chopped pecans or walnuts

4 eggs

1½ cups vegetable oil

3 cups sugar

3 cups finely shredded zucchini, drained

Two 1-ounce squares unsweetened chocolate, melted and cooled

CHOCOLATE GLAZE:

Four 1-ounce squares semisweet chocolate or ⅓ cup semisweet chocolate chips

4 tablespoons butter, softened

1 teaspoon vanilla extract

Preheat the oven to 350°F. Grease a 13 × 18-inch sheet cake pan.

To make the cake: Combine the flour, baking powder, baking soda, cinnamon, and salt. Toss ¼ cup of this flour mixture with the nuts. In a large mixing bowl, beat the eggs, oil, and sugar until light. Stir in the zucchini and chocolate, and mix well. Beat in the flour mixture just until blended and stir in the nuts. Place the mixture in the prepared pan.

Bake for 20 to 25 minutes, or until a wooden toothpick inserted in the center comes out clean. Let cool.

To make the glaze: Melt the chocolate in a microwave oven on medium-high for 30 seconds. Remove the chocolate and stir, then microwave for another 30 seconds. Stir again and repeat until the chocolate is smooth. If you use a double boiler instead, melt the chocolate over medium heat, stirring constantly until smooth. Add the butter and vanilla, and stir until smooth. Remove from the heat and cool slightly. Drizzle the glaze over the cake.

▶ *Surround yourself with the most talented people you can find, and then give them the freedom to do what they do best.*

Devil's Food Cake

MAKES ONE 9-INCH LAYER CAKE, ABOUT 8 SERVINGS

¾ cup unsweetened cocoa powder

2⅓ cups boiling water

2⅓ cups granulated sugar

¾ cup oil

⅔ cup sour cream

3 large eggs, at room temperature

2 tablespoons vanilla extract

2½ cups all purpose flour

2 tablespoons baking soda

1 teaspoon salt

1 cup chocolate chips (optional)

½ pound (2 sticks) butter, softened

3 cups confectioners' sugar

9 ounces unsweetened baking
    chocolate, melted and cooled

About ¾ cup heavy cream

Preheat the oven to 325° F. Grease and flour two 9-inch round cake pans.

Combine the cocoa powder and boiling water in a medium bowl and stir until smooth. When cool, add the granulated sugar, oil, sour cream, eggs, and 1 tablespoon of vanilla. Beat with a mixer on medium speed until blended. Reduce to low speed, then add the flour, baking soda, and salt. Beat just until smooth (the batter will be thin). Fold the chocolate chips into the batter if desired. Divide the mixture between the pans and bake for 45 to 55 minutes, or until a toothpick inserted in the center comes out clean. Cool the layers in the pans on a wire rack for 10 minutes. Run a knife around the edges of the layers, invert them onto a wire rack, and cool completely.

To make the frosting: Beat the butter and the remaining 1 tablespoon of vanilla in a large bowl with a mixer on medium speed until the butter is creamy. Reduce the speed to low and beat in ½ cup of confectioners' sugar and the melted chocolate. Alternate beating in the remaining sugar and ½ cup of cream. Increase the speed to medium and beat until spreadable. Add more cream if necessary.

Turn the layers right side up. Place 1 layer on a serving plate and spread the top with 1 cup of frosting. Add the second layer. Brush any crumbs off the cake. Coat with a thin layer of the frosting and then spread and swirl on the remaining frosting.

▶ *Because Doughmakers' 9-inch cake pan is 2¼ inches deep, it is possible to bake a layered cake in a single pan. To do this, the general rule is to lower the temperature by 25 degrees and add 15 to 20 minutes to the time.*

Diane's Double Chocolate Sheet Cake

(Texas Sheet Cake #1)

MAKES ABOUT 26 SERVINGS

When we hit the road selling our pans, ladies in the South went crazy over the size of our sheet cake pan. They said, "This will be perfect for my Texas sheet cake!" Being Rochester girls, we'd never heard of it, but after one bite, we loved this Lone Star specialty and have collected a few recipes for it along the way. —DIANE

CAKE:
3 cups flour
3 cups sugar
1½ teaspoons salt
¾ pound (3 sticks) cups butter
6 tablespoons unsweetened cocoa
1½ cups water
⅓ cup buttermilk
1½ teaspoons baking soda
1½ teaspoons vanilla extract

1½ teaspoons cinnamon
3 eggs, beaten

ICING:
4 tablespoons unsweetened cocoa
⅓ pound butter
9 tablespoons milk
5 cups confectioners' sugar
1½ teaspoons vanilla extract
1½ cups chopped pecans

Preheat the oven to 350° F. Grease a 13 × 18-inch sheet cake pan with solid vegetable shortening and lightly flour.

In a large mixing bowl, thoroughly whisk together the flour, sugar, and salt. In a heavy saucepan over medium heat, bring the butter, cocoa, and water to a boil, stirring frequently, and pour this over the sugar-flour mixture. Add the buttermilk, baking soda, vanilla, cinnamon, and eggs. Mix well and pour into the prepared pan. Bake for 30 minutes.

Apple Raspberry Pie

Overnight Cinnamon Rolls

Gingerbread Cake with Vanilla Sauce

Orange Sunshine Cake

Pecan Tassies

Nancy's Cheese Straws *(far left)* and Grandma Kramer's Old-Fashioned
Sugar, Pumpkin, and Best Oatmeal Raisin Cookies

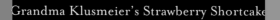
Grandma Klusmeier's Strawberry Shortcake

Red Velvet Cake

Yule Log

Winter Wonderland Bars

Maple Oat Scones

Cranberry Apple French Toast Bake

Lemon Meringue Pie

Doughmakers Soft Pretzels

Focaccia Bread

Double Chocolate Biscotti with Good Morning, Corn, and Blueberry Muffins

Ham and Dill Scones

Grilled Chicken and Sun-Dried Tomato Pizza

Almond Polenta Cake with Lemon Syrup

To make the icing: In a heavy saucepan over medium heat, bring the cocoa, butter, and milk to a rapid boil. Remove from the heat, add the confectioners' sugar, vanilla, and pecans, and beat until smooth. Spread the icing over the *hot* cake.

Allow the cake to cool slightly, then cut into 3-inch pieces.

▶ *If you buy buttermilk for a recipe and then only use a small portion of what you bought, you can freeze the rest for later baking. Measure the buttermilk into one-cup portions in freezer safe containers. After thawing, shake it before using. The texture may change, but the baking outcome shouldn't be affected.*

Joyce's Texas Sheet Cake
(Texas Sheet Cake #2)

MAKES ABOUT 20 SERVINGS

Our own Joyce McClelland offers this recipe. It is so easy, it has become a favorite at our monthly employee birthday parties.

CAKE:	ICING:
½ pound (2 sticks) margarine, softened	¾ cup milk
2 cups sugar	2 tablespoons margarine
8 eggs	3 cups sugar
2 teaspoons vanilla extract	2 cups semisweet chocolate chips
Two 16 ounce cans Hershey's chocolate syrup	1 cup chopped walnuts
2 cups flour	

Preheat the oven to 325°F. Grease a 13 × 18-inch sheet cake pan.

In a large bowl, cream together the margarine and sugar. Add the eggs and vanilla, and stir until blended. Add the chocolate syrup alternately with the flour, stirring until smooth after each addition.

Pour the batter into the prepared pan and bake for 30 minutes, or until a toothpick inserted in the center comes out clean. Cool the cake in the pan on a wire rack. Frost the cake in the pan while still warm.

To make the icing: Heat the milk in a heavy saucepan over medium heat. Melt the margarine in the milk, add the sugar, and stir to dissolve. Adjust the heat to medium-high for 30 seconds, until just boiling, then remove from the heat. Add the chocolate chips and beat by hand for 1 minute, until the chips are melted. Do not overbeat. Add the nuts, stir, and then frost the cake. Cut into 3-inch squares.

▶ *Not only is it possible to freeze nuts, but it is actually the preferred way to keep them. Most nuts will last up to six months in the freezer in sealed containers.*

Grandma Minnie's Banana Cake with Whipped Cream Frosting

MAKES ONE 9-INCH ROUND CAKE

The next two recipes are from my grandmother Minnie Baldwin, who taught me so much in the kitchen and always welcomed a small pair of hands working with her. —BETTE

1½ cups sugar

¼ pound (1 stick) butter, softened

Pinch of salt

4 ripe bananas, mashed

2 eggs, beaten

4 tablespoons sour milk (see Tip)

1 teaspoon vanilla extract

2 cups flour

1 teaspoon baking soda

FROSTING:

2 cups heavy cream

¼ cup confectioners' sugar

Preheat the oven to 350° F. Grease and flour a 9-inch round cake pan.

In a large bowl, cream together the sugar and butter. Add the salt and fold in the mashed bananas and eggs. Stir in the sour milk and vanilla.

Mix together the flour and baking soda, and add them to the banana mixture. Stir gently until just mixed in.

Pour the batter into the prepared pan and bake for 30 minutes, or until a toothpick inserted in the center comes out clean. Allow the cake to cool for 10 minutes in the pan. Run a knife around the edge of the cake and invert it onto a wire rack to cool completely.

To prepare the frosting: Pour the cream into a large mixing bowl and sprinkle in the sugar. Whip the cream with a stand mixer or hand mixer until semi-stiff peaks form, about 4 to 5 minutes.

▶ *When using recipe that calls for sour milk, you might think you have to let your milk spoil before you can bake the recipe. Not so. To make sour milk, just add ½ teaspoon of distilled vinegar to 4 tablespoons of milk and stir.*

Grandma Minnie's Date Nut Cake

MAKES ONE 9-INCH SQUARE CAKE

CAKE:

1 cup dates, quartered

1 teaspoon baking soda

1 cup boiling water

7 tablespoons butter, softened

3 tablespoons oil

1 egg

1 cup sugar

1 cup chopped walnuts

1½ cups flour

FROSTING:

8 ounces cream cheese, softened

1 teaspoon vanilla extract

3 cups confectioners' sugar

Milk

Preheat the oven to 350° F. Grease and flour a 9-inch square cake pan.

Place the dates in a medium bowl. Sprinkle with the baking soda and pour the boiling water over them. Let stand until cool. In a separate medium bowl, combine 3 tablespoons of butter, the oil, egg, and sugar. Stir in the undrained dates and walnuts. Fold in the flour. Pour the batter into the prepared pan and bake for about 30 minutes, or until a toothpick inserted in the center comes out clean.

To prepare the frosting: Use an electric mixer to combine the cream cheese, the 4 remaining tablespoons of butter, vanilla, and confectioners' sugar. Use the milk to thin the frosting to the desired consistency.

▶ *Choose a recipe you know and like, and look for any occasion to make it and share with those you love.*

Gingerbread Cake
with Vanilla Sauce

¾ cup solid vegetable shortening
⅓ pound butter, softened
1½ cups sugar
3 cups sifted flour
1½ teaspoons baking soda
¾ teaspoon baking powder
¾ teaspoon cinnamon
3 eggs, beaten
1½ cups molasses
1½ cups boiling water

VANILLA SAUCE:
1 cup sugar
2 tablespoons cornstarch
⅛ teaspoon salt
2 cups boiling water
6 tablespoons butter
2 teaspoons vanilla extract

Preheat the oven to 350° F. Grease a 9 × 13-inch pan well.

Cream the shortening and butter in a large bowl. Gradually add the sugar while continuing to beat. In a medium bowl, sift the flour, baking soda, baking powder, and cinnamon together. Add the eggs to the shortening, then add the flour mixture, molasses, and water, and beat thoroughly. Pour into the prepared pan. Bake for 30 to 40 minutes, or until a toothpick inserted in the center comes out clean.

To make the sauce: Combine the sugar, cornstarch, and salt in a heavy saucepan. Gradually pour in the boiling water and simmer over low heat, stirring constantly, for 5 minutes, or until thickened. Remove from the heat, add the butter and vanilla, and stir gently until smooth. Cool the sauce to lukewarm and drizzle over gingerbread cake.

▶ *Don't be afraid of competition; it is simply the way the marketplace works. If you distinguish your product and service from all the rest, you will find a way.*

Italian Cream Cake

MAKES ONE 9-INCH ROUND LAYER CAKE

A prizewinning recipe from the 2003 Doughmakers Baking Contest, submitted by Jean Ann Shell, Terre Haute, Indiana.

CAKE:

¼ pound (1 stick) butter

¼ cup applesauce

¼ cup solid vegetable shortening

2 cups sugar

1¼ cups Egg Beaters

2 cups flour

¼ teaspoon salt

1 teaspoon baking soda

2 cups shredded coconut

1 scant cup milk plus 2 tablespoons lemon juice or 1 cup buttermilk

1 cup chopped pecans

1¼ cups liquid egg whites, stiffly beaten until peaks form

1 teaspoon vanilla extract

1 teaspoon almond extract

ICING:

One 8-ounce package cream cheese or fat-free cream cheese, at room temperature

¼ pound (1 stick) butter, at room temperature

1 pound confectioners' sugar

1 teaspoon vanilla extract

1 cup chopped pecans

Preheat the oven to 350° F. Grease and lightly flour three 9-inch round cake pans.

In a large bowl, combine the butter, applesauce, shortening, and sugar. Add the Egg Beaters a little at a time, beating after each addition. In a medium bowl, mix together the flour, salt, baking soda, and coconut. Alternately add the flour mixture and milk to the butter, stirring after each addition. Stir in the pecans. Fold in the beaten egg whites and vanilla and almond extracts. Pour the batter evenly into the prepared cake pans and bake for 30 minutes, or until a toothpick inserted in the center comes out clean. Allow the cakes to cool on a wire rack for about 30 minutes.

To make the icing: Beat together the cream cheese and butter. Add the confectioners' sugar and vanilla, and mix until smooth. Stir in the pecans, reserving 2 tablespoons.

Assemble the cake in 3 layers with icing between each layer. Ice the top and sides of the cake and sprinkle the remaining pecans on top. Keep refrigerated and serve cool.

▶ *The secret to perfectly beaten egg whites: Start beating vigorously with an electric mixer, balloon whisk, or rotary egg beater. Keep whisking while you add sugar or other ingredients as directed. Egg whites are ready when they just barely hold a peak. Check for doneness before you think they're ready. You can always beat them longer, but you can't unbeat them.*

Nanie's Pound Cake

MAKES 2 CAKES

This recipe comes from Olga Anderssen McLaughlin, my husband Brooks's grandmother, who emigrated from Sweden in 1922. —BETTE

1 pound (1 stick) butter, softened
4 cups sugar
9 extra-large eggs
Grated zest of 2 oranges
2 teaspoons vanilla extract
8 cups sifted all-purpose flour
1 cup raisins, tossed in flour

Preheat the oven to 275° F. Grease and lightly flour two 8½ × 4½-inch loaf pans.

Beat the butter in a large mixing bowl until creamy. Add the sugar and beat for 20 minutes. With the machine running, add the eggs, 1 at a time, beating thoroughly after each addition. Add the orange zest and vanilla, and mix until blended. With a spoon, fold in the flour a little at a time until the batter is smooth, then fold in the floured raisins.

Pour the batter into the prepared pans and bake for about 1 hour and 50 minutes, or until lightly golden on top. Let the cakes cool completely in the pans, about 1 to 2 hours. Loosen the edges with a thin knife before turning the cake out. This cake is rich and moist enough to serve plain.

▶ *Work at being a friend, and you will have many for yourself.*

Walnut-Glazed Brown Sugar Pound Cake

MAKES 12 TO 15 SERVINGS

½ pound (2 sticks) butter, softened
½ cup solid vegetable shortening
2 cups brown sugar
1 cup granulated sugar
5 eggs
3 cups all-purpose flour
1 teaspoon baking powder
½ teaspoon salt
1 cup evaporated milk
1 teaspoon vanilla extract

½ teaspoon maple flavoring
1 cup chopped walnuts

WALNUT GLAZE:
1 cup confectioners' sugar
2 tablespoons butter, softened
6 tablespoons evaporated milk
1 teaspoon vanilla extract

½ cup chopped walnuts

Preheat the oven to 325° F. Grease and flour a 10-inch tube pan or two 8½ × 4½-inch loaf pans.

Cream the butter, shortening, brown sugar, and granulated sugar in a large mixing bowl. Add the eggs, 1 at a time, beating after each addition. In a medium bowl, sift together the flour, baking powder, and salt. In another bowl, mix together the milk, vanilla, and maple flavoring. Alternately add the flour mixture and the milk mixture to the creamed butter, mixing after each addition. Fold in the walnuts and pour the mixture into the prepared pan. Bake for 1 hour and 15 minutes, or until a toothpick inserted in the center comes out clean.

Meanwhile, make the glaze: Beat together the confectioners' sugar, butter, milk, and vanilla until smooth.

Remove the cake from the oven and allow to cool in the pan for 10 to 15 minutes. Drizzle with the glaze and sprinkle the chopped walnuts on top.

▶ *Be wary of your competition. Decide early on what your trade secrets are and keep them safe. Before sharing any information with a competitor, ask yourself, "If he breaks trust or acts in bad faith, how can the information I share be used against me?"*

Chocolate Sour Cream Pound Cake

MAKES 1 LOAF

1 cup boiling water

Two 1-ounce squares unsweetened
   chocolate, chopped into small
   pieces

2 cups sifted all-purpose flour

¼ teaspoon salt

1 teaspoon baking soda

¼ pound (1 stick) butter, softened

1¾ cups firmly packed light
   brown sugar

2 eggs

1 teaspoon vanilla extract

½ cup sour cream

Confectioners' sugar for dusting

Preheat the oven to 325°F. Grease and flour an 8½ × 4½-inch loaf pan.

In a small bowl, pour the boiling water over the chocolate and stir to melt it. Allow to cool.

In a large bowl, stir together the flour, salt, and baking soda. In another large bowl, cream together the butter and sugar. Add the eggs and vanilla, continuing to beat as you add each ingredient.

Add half of the flour mixture to the butter-sugar mixture and beat thoroughly. Add the sour cream and continue beating. Add the remaining flour mixture and beat until combined. Add the chocolate mixture and beat until just blended.

Pour the batter into the prepared loaf pan. Bake for about 1 hour to 1 hour 15 minutes, until a tester inserted in the center comes out clean. Remove from the oven and cool in the pan on a wire rack for 15 minutes. Run a thin knife around the edge of the cake and remove from the pan. Continue cooling the cake on the wire rack. Dust with confectioners' sugar before slicing.

▶ *Mind your business. Don't turn over so much control of day-to-day operations that you don't know what the near-term goals and challenges are.*

Oatmeal Cake

MAKES 15 SERVINGS

A prizewinning recipe from the 2003 Doughmakers Baking Contest, submitted by Judy Abbinett, Terre Haute, Indiana.

CAKE:
1¼ cups boiling water
1 cup quick oats
1 teaspoon baking soda
¼ pound (1 stick) butter, at
    room temperature
1 cup granulated sugar
1 cup packed brown sugar
2 eggs
1⅓ cups sifted flour
½ teaspoon cinnamon

TOPPING:
6 tablespoons butter, melted
½ cup brown sugar
¼ cup evaporated milk or cream
1 cup coconut
½ cup chopped nuts
½ teaspoon vanilla extract

Preheat the oven to 350° F. Grease a 9 × 13-inch cake pan.

In a medium bowl, pour the boiling water over the quick oats and stir. Stir in the baking soda and let stand for 20 minutes. In a large bowl, cream together the butter and sugars. Mix in the eggs, flour, and cinnamon. Fold in the oat mixture and mix well.

Pour into the prepared pan and bake for 35 minutes, or until golden brown.

While the cake is baking, prepare the topping by gently mixing the melted butter with the brown sugar and milk in a small bowl. Add the coconut, nuts, and vanilla, and mix well. Spread the topping mixture on the cake while it is still warm. Place under a broiler set to high until the icing is bubbling and brown, about 1 minute. Watch it carefully and allow to cool before slicing.

▶ *Toothpicks are often too short to reach the center of a cake for testing, so try a piece of dry spaghetti instead.*

Orange Sunshine Cake

MAKES ABOUT 12 TO 15 SERVINGS

Aunt Jessie was my grandfather's sister, and I remember her for her bright red hair. She and Uncle George never had children, and when I was born, I became her special girl. I remember our making this cake together many times. I loved baking with Aunt Jess, and I think you'll enjoy this delicious light cake. —BETTE

5 eggs, separated

1½ cups sugar, sifted 4 times
before measuring

1 teaspoon salt

3½ tablespoons cold water

1 teaspoon orange extract

1½ tablespoons orange juice

Grated zest of 1 orange

½ teaspoon cream of tartar

1¾ cups cake flour, sifted
4 times before measuring

Preheat the oven to 350°F. Grease and flour an angel food or tube cake pan.

Beat the yolks lightly with a whisk. Add the sugar, a little at a time, and beat vigorously. Stir in the salt, water, orange extract, juice, and zest. Set aside. Beat the egg whites until frothy. Add the cream of tartar and continue beating until soft peaks form. Set aside. Slowly blend the flour into the egg yolk mixture. Gently fold in the egg whites. Pour the batter into the prepared pan.

Bake for 48 to 55 minutes, or until a tester inserted in the center comes out clean.

Allow the cake to cool for 5 minutes in the pan, then run a thin knife around the edge to loosen the cake. Invert it onto a serving platter.

▶ *Get the most out of your lemon or orange zest by adding it when you cream the butter and sugar together.*

Pumpkin Cake Roll

MAKES ABOUT 8 TO 10 SERVINGS

CAKE:

3 eggs

1 cup granulated sugar

⅔ cup canned pumpkin

1 teaspoon lemon juice

¾ cup flour

1 teaspoon baking powder

½ teaspoon salt

½ teaspoon ginger

½ teaspoon nutmeg

2 teaspoons cinnamon

1 cup finely chopped walnuts

FILLING:

1 cup confectioners' sugar, plus
    1 tablespoon for sprinkling

Two 3-ounce packages cream
    cheese, softened

4 tablespoons butter, softened

½ teaspoon vanilla extract

Preheat the oven to 375° F. Grease and flour a 10 × 15-inch jelly roll pan.

In a large bowl, beat the eggs on high speed for 5 minutes. Gradually beat in the granulated sugar and stir in the pumpkin and lemon juice. In a separate bowl, mix together the flour, baking powder, salt, ginger, nutmeg, and cinnamon. Fold into the pumpkin mixture. Spread in the prepared pan. Top with the walnuts and bake for 15 minutes, or until a tester inserted in the center comes out clean.

To make the filling: Mix together the 1 cup of confectioners' sugar, cream cheese, butter, and vanilla until smooth.

While the cake is still warm, turn it out onto a towel sprinkled with confectioners' sugar. Starting at the narrow end, roll the towel and cake together. Let cool. Unroll the cake and top it with filling, then reroll and chill.

▶ *When you get a flat tire, call AAA, and then change it yourself. You'll probably be cleaning up and ready to hit the road again by the time "help" arrives.*

Praline Turtle Cake

MAKES 16 SERVINGS

This recipe, submitted by Betty Nicoson of Terre Haute, Indiana, won first prize in the cake division at the 2003 Doughmakers Baking Contest.

¼ pound (1 stick) butter

1 cup brown sugar

1 can sweetened condensed milk

1 cup chopped pecans

2 cups flour

¾ cup unsweetened cocoa

2 cups granulated sugar

1½ teaspoons baking powder

1½ teaspoons baking soda

1 teaspoon salt

2 eggs

1 cup sour cream

½ cup oil

1 cup hot water

1 teaspoon vanilla extract

1 teaspoon vinegar

1 small jar fudge topping (about ½ cup)

½ cup chocolate chips

Chocolate frosting (1 can of your favorite brand)

Preheat the oven to 350°F. Cut 2 sheets of parchment paper to fit two 9-inch round cake pans and place them in the pans.

Melt the butter, brown sugar, and milk in a 2-quart saucepan over medium heat. Do not boil. Pour even portions into the cake pans. Sprinkle ¾ cup of the pecans evenly over mixture in the pans. Set aside.

In a large mixing bowl, mix together the flour, cocoa, granulated sugar, baking powder, baking soda, and salt. Add the eggs, sour cream, oil, hot water, vanilla, and vinegar, and stir until well blended. Spoon evenly over the mixture in the pans.

Bake for 35 to 40 minutes, or until a toothpick inserted in the center comes out clean. Cool the cake for 10 minutes, then loosen it by running a knife around the edges. Turn the pans over onto cooling racks and let cool completely. Remove the parchment paper from the cake to expose the praline topping.

Spread the fudge topping on one cake layer. Place the other layer on top so that the fudge is in the middle and there is a layer of praline on top.

Place the chocolate chips in a microwave-safe bowl and microwave on medium for 30 seconds. Stir and repeat until smooth. Drizzle over the top of the cake. Sprinkle with the remaining pecans. To add the finishing touch, frost only the sides of the cake with your favorite chocolate frosting.

▶ *One of the hardest things for would-be entrepreneurs to do is believe in themselves, but it is this faith that separates the dreamers from the doers.*

Red Velvet Cake

MAKES 8 SERVINGS

¼ pound (1 stick) butter, softened

1½ cups sugar

2 eggs

2 ounces red food coloring

2 tablespoons unsweetened cocoa

2½ cups cake flour

1 cup buttermilk

1 teaspoon salt

1 teaspoon vanilla extract

1 teaspoon baking soda dissolved in
   1 tablespoon vinegar

FROSTING:

¼ pound (1 stick) butter, softened

8 ounces cream cheese, softened

3 tablespoons milk

4 to 5 cups confectioners' sugar

Preheat the oven to 350°F. Grease two 9-inch round cake pans with solid vegetable shortening and then lightly flour them.

Cream together the butter, sugar, and eggs in a large bowl. Add the food coloring and cocoa. Alternately add half of the cake flour, half of the buttermilk, and half of the salt. Mix after each addition and then repeat. Stir in the vanilla. Fold in the baking soda and vinegar. Pour the mixture evenly into the prepared pans and bake for 30 minutes, or until a toothpick inserted in the center comes out clean.

Allow the cakes to cool slightly in the pans, about 10 minutes. Loosen the sides by running a thin knife along the edge of the pans. Turn the cakes out onto a wire rack and allow to cool completely.

To make the frosting: Cream together the butter, cream cheese, and milk. Add the confectioners' sugar until you reach the desired consistency. Additional milk can be used to thin the frosting if needed.

Place the bottom layer on a cake base and frost the top. Place the second layer on the first, then frost the top and sides.

▶ *Don't be afraid to wear many hats when you start your company. They won't all fit perfectly; some may feel silly, and some may be too big. But as you grow, you can wear the ones that look good on you and then find employees or partners to wear the other ones.*

Easy Cut and Serve Cheesecake

MAKES 16 TO 24 SLICES

1 package lemon Jell-O
1 package unflavored gelatin
1 cup water
Two 16-ounces packages Cool
    Whip, thawed
1 cup milk

Three 8-ounce packages cream
    cheese, softened
1½ cups plus 3 tablespoons sugar
1½ packages graham crackers,
    crumbled
6 tablespoons butter, melted

In a small saucepan over medium-high heat, stir the Jell-O and gelatin into the water and bring to a boil, stirring occasionally. Remove from the heat and allow to cool. Meanwhile, beat the Cool Whip with the milk until blended. In another bowl, beat the cream cheese thoroughly, then add 1½ cups of sugar and mix until creamy. Add the gelatin mixture, stir, and then stir in the Cool Whip.

To make the crust: In a medium bowl, mix the graham crackers with the melted butter and the remaining 3 tablespoons of sugar until uniform and crumbly. Press the crumbs into a greased 9 × 13-inch cake pan and up the sides as much as possible. Pour the cheesecake mixture on top of the crust. Chill in the refrigerator for several hours, until set, or overnight.

▶ *Keeping a knife blade clean and warm makes it easier to cut neat servings from your cakes, so dip your knife into a wine cooler filled with hot water and wipe it on a clean towel between slices.*

Mini Cheesecakes

MAKES 4 DOZEN

One 12-ounce package vanilla wafers
Two 8-ounce packages cream cheese, softened
¾ cup sugar
2 eggs
1 teaspoon vanilla extract
One 21-ounce can cherry pie filling (see Tip)

Preheat the oven to 350°F. Line two 24-cup mini muffin pans with paper liners.

Put the vanilla wafers in a food processor and pulse until finely ground. Place ½ teaspoon of crushed wafers in the bottom of each paper cup.

In the large bowl of an electric mixer, beat the cream cheese, sugar, eggs, and vanilla on medium speed until light and fluffy, about 10 minutes. Fill each muffin liner about ¾ full with this mixture. With the back of a teaspoon, make an indention in the center of the batter and put 1 teaspoon of pie filling in the space.

Bake for 15 minutes, or until the tops just begin to brown.

▶ *Cherry pie filling is a classic flavor, but you can substitute other fruit fillings or even fruit preserves.*

Sour Cream Spice Cake

MAKES SIXTEEN 2-INCH SERVINGS

2 cups sugar

2 eggs

1 tablespoon butter,
softened

2 teaspoons baking soda

1 cup sour milk*

1 cup sour cream

1 teaspoon cloves

2 tablespoons unsweetened
cocoa

1 tablespoon cinnamon

3 cups flour

Preheat the oven to 350°F. Grease and flour a 9 × 13-inch cake pan.

Cream together the sugar, eggs, and butter. Dissolve the baking soda in the sour milk, then add it with the sour cream to the egg mixture and stir. Add the cloves, cocoa, and cinnamon, and mix well. Add the flour and mix until the batter is well blended. Pour the batter into the prepared pan and bake for 40 to 45 minutes, or until a toothpick inserted in the center comes out clean.

*To make sour milk, add 1 tablespoon of vinegar or lemon juice to 1 cup of milk.

▶ *If the corporate world seems cold and uncaring, remember that it doesn't have to be that way. You can set the tone for your company.*

Yule Log

MAKES 10 SERVINGS

SPONGE CAKE:

6 egg yolks

1 cup sugar

¾ teaspoon vanilla extract

6 egg whites

1 cup sifted cake flour

1½ teaspoons baking powder

⅜ teaspoon salt

¼ cup sifted confectioners' sugar

CHOCOLATE BUTTERCREAM:

12 tablespoons (1½ sticks) butter, softened

2 pounds sifted confectioners' sugar

Scant ½ cup light cream

1 tablespoon vanilla extract

4 ounces unsweetened chocolate, melted and cooled

Preheat the oven to 375°F. Butter and flour a 10 × 15-inch jelly roll pan.

Beat the egg yolks until thick and lemon-colored. Gradually beat in ¼ cup of sugar, then stir in the vanilla. In another bowl, beat the egg whites until soft peaks form. Gradually beat in the remaining ¾ cup of sugar and beat until stiff peaks form. Fold the yolks into the whites. Sift together the cake flour, baking powder, and salt, and fold into the egg mixture. Spread evenly in the prepared pan. Bake for 12 to 15 minutes, or until done. Immediately loosen the sides and turn the cake out onto a towel sprinkled with sifted confectioners' sugar. Roll the cake and towel together and place them on a rack to cool.

To make the buttercream: In a medium bowl, cream the butter and gradually add about half of the sugar. Beat in 4 tablespoons of cream, the vanilla, and cooled chocolate. Gradually blend in the remaining sugar (reserving a little for dusting the cake) and enough cream to reach spreading consistency.

Unroll the sponge cake and towel, and place the cake on a clean surface. Spread ⅔ of the buttercream on it. Roll the cake. Place the roll on a serving platter and cover with the buttercream, making the surface look rough, like bark. Sift the sugar lightly over the entire roll to look like a dusting of snow. Decorate with fresh or artificial holly, evergreens, or other holiday trim.

VARIATION: Fill the cake with a red berry filling, ice it with a white buttercream, and sprinkle it with clear edible glitter to give it a frosty look. Or, to save calories, ice the cake with whipped topping, and then be sure to refrigerate it until ready to serve.

▶ *One good knife may cost you more than an entire set of cheap knives. There are reasons for this, and we think it is worth the investment.*

Cookies

Alva's Spritz Cookies

MAKES ABOUT 6 DOZEN

1 cup solid vegetable
    shortening or ½ cup
    butter and ½ cup
    shortening
¾ cup sugar

1 egg
1 teaspoon vanilla extract
2¼ cups sifted flour
¼ teaspoon salt
½ teaspoon baking powder

In a large mixing bowl, cream together the shortening and sugar until light and fluffy. Add the egg and vanilla, and mix to combine. Sift the flour with the salt and baking powder, and gradually beat in the butter-sugar mixture until it makes a smooth dough. Wrap the dough in plastic and refrigerate for 1 to 2 hours or overnight.

Preheat the oven to 375°F.

Spoon the dough into a cookie press and press the dough directly onto an ungreased cookie sheet in the desired shape or design. Bake on the middle rack of the oven for 10 to 12 minutes, or until they just begin to brown.

▶ *Invest in quality. Use only uncoated solid aluminum baking sheets and pans, preferably those with a textured surface. We know a good company that makes them!*

Best Oatmeal Raisin Cookie

MAKES ABOUT 4 DOZEN

Offered by Colleen Austin, Madison Heights, Michigan.

1½ cups all purpose flour
1 cup firmly packed dark brown sugar
½ cup sugar
1 teaspoon baking soda
1 teaspoon cinnamon
¼ teaspoon ground ginger
¼ teaspoon nutmeg
½ teaspoon salt

½ cup butter flavored solid vegetable shortening
¼ pound (1 stick) margarine, softened
2 eggs
1 teaspoon vanilla extract
3 cups old-fashioned uncooked oats
1 cup raisins

Preheat the oven to 350°F.

In a large bowl, stir together the flour, sugars, baking soda, cinnamon, ginger, nutmeg, and salt until they are well combined. In another large bowl, cream together the shortening and margarine. Add the eggs and vanilla, and beat well. Gradually add the flour mixture and beat well after each addition. Add the oats and raisins, and stir until evenly mixed in. Using a cookie scoop or a tablespoon, drop the dough onto an ungreased cookie sheet about 1 inch apart.

Bake for 11 to 12 minutes, or until the tops are light brown. Cool the cookies for 1 minute on the cookie sheet, then transfer them to a wire rack and let cool completely (if you can wait that long).

▶ *Let the kids help you in the kitchen—your own or someone else's. The mess is bigger and it takes longer, but it is so much more fun. And they will remember baking with you.*

Denise's Old-Fashioned Sour Cream Cookies

MAKES 4 TO 5 DOZEN

Some of my new friends after I moved to Terre Haute were Denise and her daughter, Crystal. One time Denise brought these cookies to our Bible study, and they quickly became a favorite. —BETTE

1 cup margarine, softened	1 teaspoon baking powder
1½ cups sugar	1 teaspoon salt
2 eggs	½ teaspoon nutmeg
4½ cups flour	1 cup sour cream
1 teaspoon baking soda	1 teaspoon vanilla extract

In the large bowl of an electric mixer, cream together the margarine and sugar until light and fluffy. Add the eggs, 1 at a time, and mix on medium speed after each addition, until well blended. In a large mixing bowl, whisk or sift together the flour, baking soda, baking powder, salt, and nutmeg. Add to the mixer, a little at a time, and continue beating on medium speed. When about half the flour mixture has been added, add ½ cup of sour cream and the vanilla, and continue mixing until blended. Add the remaining flour mixture, a little at a time, and finish with the remaining sour cream. Mix until a soft dough forms. Turn the dough out onto a work surface and shape into a mounded disk. Cover with plastic wrap and chill for at least 1 hour.

Preheat the oven to 375°F. Roll the chilled dough out to ¼ inch thick and cut into desired shapes. Bake for 12 minutes, or until the edges just begin to brown.

▶ *Be a compassionate business owner. Let your employees work half-days, and tell them you don't care what they do with the other twelve hours.*

Depression Cookies

MAKES ABOUT 6 DOZEN

My mother made these cookies back in the early '40s, and since then this recipe has been handed back and forth between friends. During the Depression, raisins were given to families as "commodities," along with other staples such as flour, cornmeal, dried beans, peanut butter, lard, and prunes. My brother and I called these poor people's Fig Newtons. —MARY J. SCULLY, SULLIVAN, INDIANA

FILLING:
1½ cups finely chopped raisins
¾ cup sugar
2 tablespoons flour
1 cup warm water

DOUGH:
1½ cups sugar
¼ pound (1 stick) butter, softened

½ cup milk
1 egg
1 teaspoon vanilla extract
3 teaspoons baking powder
½ teaspoon salt
4½ cups flour, plus additional for
   dusting

Place all the filling ingredients in a heavy saucepan over medium-high heat and simmer until virtually all the liquid has been absorbed or evaporated, about 10 minutes. Remove from the heat and allow mixture to cool.

Preheat the oven to 350°F.

To make the dough: In a large mixing bowl, cream together the sugar and butter. Add the milk, egg, and vanilla, and beat well. In another large bowl, stir together the baking powder, salt, and flour. Add to the butter mixture, a little at a time, and mix well to form a smooth dough.

Roll the dough out to about ¼ inch thick on a floured work surface and cut with a 2-inch round biscuit cutter. Place 1 teaspoon of the filling on each round and fold the dough in half. Seal the seams by pressing with the tines of a fork. Prick the cookies with the fork; this will allow the steam to release during baking. Arrange the cookies on an ungreased cookie sheet and bake for 10 to 12 minutes.

▶ *Always cool your cookies for 2 to 3 minutes on the pan before removing them to a wire rack to cool completely.*

Double Chocolate Biscotti

MAKES ABOUT 90 TO 100

Chef Steven Douglas Keneipp of The Classic Kitchen in Noblesville, Indiana, offers this recipe for biscotti. Steve was trained by our friend Dr. Fredericka Kramer and carries our bakeware in his shop.—BETTE

4½ cups unbleached white flour

1 tablespoon baking powder

½ teaspoon salt

½ cup unsweetened Dutch-process cocoa

4 tablespoons unsalted butter, softened

2 cups sugar

4 eggs

2 egg whites

2 teaspoons vanilla extract

4 teaspoons almond extract

¼ cup Amaretto liqueur or brewed coffee

1½ cups coarsely chopped almonds

1 cup mini chocolate chips or finely chopped bittersweet chocolate

Preheat the oven to 350°F. Place the rack in the middle of the oven. Line 2 large baking sheets or jelly roll pans with parchment paper.

In a large bowl, sift together the flour, baking powder, salt, and cocoa. In the large bowl of an electric mixer, beat together the butter and sugar until it creates a uniform crumb. Add the eggs and egg whites, 1 at a time, mixing well after each addition. Beat in the vanilla and almond extracts and liqueur until well combined.

Turn off the mixer, add the flour mixture, and mix at the lowest speed until blended. Scrape down the sides, then fold in the almonds and chocolate chips by hand.

Turn the dough out onto a work surface and gather it into a ball. Add a little more flour if it is too sticky to handle. Divide the dough into quarters. Form each quarter into an elongated mound about 12 × 4 inches. Place the mounds on the prepared baking sheets (2 per sheet) about 3 inches apart.

Bake for 20 to 25 minutes, until the dough is dry on top and firm to the touch. Remove the dough from the oven, transfer to a wire rack, and allow to cool for 5 minutes.

Lower the oven temperature to 300°F. With a serrated knife, slice the dough into pieces about 4 × ½ inch. Place, cut side down, on the original lined baking sheets and bake for another 15 to 20 minutes, until crisp and dry. Remove to wire racks to cool. The biscotti may be stored for several days in an airtight container.

▶ *Biscotti will often crumble when you slice them. To minimize this, after the first baking, cool the log of dough, wrap it, and freeze it overnight. Slice it frozen with a sharp knife, allow it to thaw, and then put it in the oven for the second baking.*

Grandma Kramer's Old-Fashioned Sugar Cookies

MAKES 3 TO 4 DOZEN

Each holiday Mom made these cookies for me and my two brothers to take to school to share with friends. This was around 1944 when I was twelve years old. I thought I was too old to take cookies to school, but when I acted as if I didn't have any, my friends would pester me until I produced them. Our family still expects them every holiday. —DON KRAMER, LINTON, INDIANA

½ pound butter (2 sticks), at room temperature

3 cups sugar

3 eggs

6½ cups flour

½ teaspoon salt

2 teaspoons baking powder

½ teaspoon nutmeg

1 teaspoon baking soda

1 cup buttermilk

2 tablespoons vanilla extract

Sugar for decorating

Icing (optional)

In a large bowl, cream together the butter and sugar with a mixer. Add the eggs and mix thoroughly. In a separate bowl, sift together the flour, salt, baking powder, and nutmeg. In a third bowl, dissolve the baking soda in the buttermilk and add vanilla. Add the flour mixture alternately with the buttermilk to the creamed butter, using the mixer until you get to the last 2 cups of flour. Then use a wooden spoon to mix in the remaining flour to create a soft dough. Divide the dough into thirds and form into balls. Cover with plastic wrap and chill overnight. You may keep the dough for a couple of days in the refrigerator.

Preheat the oven to 375°F.

Taking 1 ball of dough at a time, roll it out on a lightly floured surface to about a ¼-inch thickness. Cut with cookie cutters and arrange on an ungreased baking sheet.

Bake for 8 to 10 minutes, watching the cookies carefully. Remove them as soon as the edges just begin to brown. Sprinkle with sugar while they are still warm or top with icing after they have cooled. Repeat with the remaining dough if desired.

▶ *Customer complaints may seem like an unpleasant reality in business life, but you can learn to see them as opportunities. If you take customers' complaints seriously and respond with more than they ask for in an effort to make matters right, you can win them over to being loyal and enthusiastic customers for life.*

Hot Chocolate Earthquakes

MAKES ABOUT 4½ DOZEN

6 ounces (1½ sticks) butter

⅔ cup unsweetened cocoa

¾ cup plus ⅓ cup granulated
sugar

¾ cup firmly packed brown
sugar

¼ teaspoon hot red cayenne
pepper

¾ teaspoon salt

2 large eggs

2 cups all-purpose flour

1½ teaspoons baking soda

½ cup semisweet chocolate chips

Preheat the oven to 375°F.

Heat the butter in a large saucepan over medium heat until just melted. Remove from the heat and whisk in the cocoa, ¾ cup of the granulated and brown sugars, the cayenne, and salt until smooth. Stir in the eggs. Sift the flour and baking soda into the saucepan and stir until completely blended. Stir in the chocolate chips.

Turn the dough out of the saucepan onto parchment or waxed paper on the work surface. If the dough is too soft to work with, cover and chill it until firm. Form the dough into 1-inch balls and roll them in the ⅓ cup of sugar. Arrange the balls 2 inches apart on ungreased cookie sheets.

Bake the cookies for 10 to 12 minutes, or until the tops are cracked. The cookies will be very soft. Do not bake longer, or they will lose their chewiness. Let the cookies cool completely on the sheets and then serve them or transfer them to airtight containers.

▶ *For holiday baking, work with at least three cookie sheets: one for setting up, one for baking, and one for cooling.*

Nancy's Cheese Straws

MAKES ABOUT 65 CHEESE STRAWS

6 ounces (1½ sticks) butter, melted
¾ pound extra sharp cheddar cheese, finely grated
¼ to ½ teaspoon cayenne pepper
¼ teaspoon medium ground black pepper (optional)
½ teaspoon salt
2 cups flour

Preheat the oven to 350°F.

In a large bowl, pour the butter over the cheese while the butter is still hot. Mix the cheese and butter with a mixer until blended. Add the cayenne, black pepper, if desired, and salt. Add the flour, a little at a time, mixing well after each addition until a soft dough forms.

Spoon the dough into a cookie press or gun fitted with a tip that will make strips. Or load a pastry bag with a star-burst tip. Press the dough out onto an ungreased cookie sheet to form 2-inch strips.

Bake the cheese straws for 20 minutes, watching carefully, until lightly browned or a dark golden color. Cool on the baking sheet for a few minutes, then transfer to a wire rack. These can be stored for up to 1 week in an airtight container, or they may be frozen for a month.

▶ *If at all possible, launch your product or service as the first in a new category. We were able to launch the first brand of "textured bakeware." That's much better than being a new brand in a crowded field.*

Peanut Butter Oatmeal Chocolate Chip Cookies

MAKES 6 DOZEN

½ pound (2 sticks) butter, at room temperature

2 cups packed brown sugar

2 cups granulated sugar

4 teaspoons baking soda

2 tablespoons vanilla extract

3 cups peanut butter, creamy or chunky

6 eggs, beaten

9 cups quick-cooking rolled oats

One 16-ounce package chocolate chips

Preheat the oven to 350°F.

Cream the butter and sugars together in a large mixing bowl. Add the baking soda, vanilla, peanut butter, and eggs, and mix well. Add the oats and mix until well blended. Fold the chocolate chips into the dough. Drop the dough by rounded tablespoons, 2 inches apart, onto an ungreased cookie sheet. Bake for 10 minutes. The cookies should be soft and lightly browned.

▶ *A shiny aluminum baking sheet will give you the best results for virtually every kind of cookie. They bake evenly and give that light golden color that is so appealing for baked goods.*

Sealed with a Kiss Cookies

MAKES ABOUT 4 DOZEN

Offered by Clarice Duits, Indianapolis, Indiana.

4 tablespoons butter

One 12-ounce package semisweet chocolate chips

One 14-ounce can sweetened condensed milk

1 teaspoon vanilla extract

2 cups all-purpose flour

45 Hershey's Kisses, unwrapped

10 ounces chocolate-flavored bark coating, broken
   into chunks

Preheat the oven to 350°F.

Combine the butter and chocolate chips in a 4-quart mixing bowl. Microwave on high for 30 seconds, then stir. Repeat until the mixture is smooth and creamy. Add the condensed milk and mix well. Stir in the vanilla. Add the flour, 1 cup at a time, stirring after each addition, until the dough is smooth and evenly blended.

Make cookie dough balls using a 1-inch cookie scoop. Place a Hershey's Kiss in the middle of each cookie and wrap the dough evenly around it, covering it except for the very tip and forming a ball.

Bake about 2 inches apart on an ungreased cookie sheet for 10 minutes. Let the cookies cool on the baking sheet for about 5 minutes, then remove from the baking sheet and let cool completely. The cookies can be frozen at this point for up to a month. Remove from the freezer and allow to thaw before dipping in the chocolate bark.

Break up the chocolate bark and zap in the microwave on high for 20 seconds, then stir. Repeat until the bark is smooth and creamy. Dip the top of each cookie in the melted bark. Allow the cookies to set at room temperature until the bark is firm. If the dipping bark in the bowl begins to get hard as you work with it, heat it in the microwave for 20 seconds and stir before continuing.

▶ *The difference between bittersweet and semisweet chocolate is the amount of chocolate liquor. Bittersweet chocolate has more and therefore has a stronger flavor. Depending on your taste, they can be used interchangeably.*

Sugar Cookie Cutouts

MAKES ABOUT 3 DOZEN

⅓ pound butter, at room
   temperature
2 eggs
1 teaspoon vanilla extract
1 cup sugar
¼ cup milk
3½ cups flour
1 teaspoon baking soda
1 teaspoon salt

ICING:
¼ pound (1 stick) butter, at
   room temperature
1 pound confectioners' sugar
3 tablespoons milk
1 teaspoon vanilla extract
Food coloring (optional)

Preheat the oven to 350°F.

Blend together the butter, eggs, vanilla, sugar, and milk. Add the flour, baking soda, and salt. Mix together well and form into a ball of dough. Cover with plastic wrap and refrigerate at least 30 minutes. Roll out to a ⅛-inch thickness and cut into desired shapes.

Bake for 8 to 10 minutes on an ungreased cookie sheet. Watch carefully and remove the cookies when the edges begin to brown slightly. Don't let the tops brown. Cool the cookies on a wire rack before icing and decorating.

To make the icing: Blend the butter, sugar, milk, and vanilla until smooth and creamy. If you want to color the icing, transfer a small amount to another bowl, add the food coloring, and mix until you get the desired color. Spread on the cutout cookies and decorate as desired.

▶ *When baking for the holidays, try preparing several different dough recipes on one day and then shape and bake the cookies on another day. This makes the work more manageable when you're doing a lot of baking.*

Swedish Red Lips

MAKES ABOUT 4 DOZEN

This is another recipe from my husband's grandmother, Olga McLaughlin. The currants, which are plentiful in Sweden, and the family connection are what distinguish this recipe from other thumbprint cookies. They have become something of a signature for Doughmakers because we make them at the gourmet trade shows. The retail buyers and other exhibitors flock to our booth to have one. And, naturally, while they are visiting, we try to sell them on stocking our product. —BETTE

½ pound (2 sticks) butter, softened
½ cup sugar
2 cups flour
1 jar red currant jelly

Preheat the oven to 375°F.

Mix the butter and sugar with a hand mixer until very light and fluffy. Add the flour gradually and blend thoroughly. Refrigerate the dough until easy to handle, about 1 hour. Form the dough into olive-sized balls. Make a dimple in each ball with your thumb and fill it with a little jelly.

Bake on an ungreased cookie sheet for 10 to 15 minutes, or until they just begin to turn golden around the edges.

▶ *The round handle end of a wooden spoon or the eraser end of a pencil covered with plastic wrap work well for making dimples in thumbprint cookies.*

Swedish Tea Cakes

MAKES ABOUT 50

½ pound (2 sticks) margarine, softened
2½ cups confectioners' sugar
2 teaspoons vanilla extract
2 cups all-purpose flour
¼ teaspoon salt
1 cup finely chopped almonds or pecans

Preheat the oven to 325°F.

In a mixing bowl, cream the margarine, ½ cup of sugar, and the vanilla. Blend in the flour, salt, and nuts until the dough holds together. Shape into 1-inch balls and place them 1 inch apart on an ungreased baking sheet. Bake for 15 to 20 minutes, or until the cookies are set but not brown. Cool for 5 minutes, then roll in the remaining 2 cups of sugar. Cool the cookies completely and roll them again in the sugar.

▶ *Some cookies freeze well, but when possible, freeze your dough and bake as needed. Nothing beats the taste or smell of fresh from-the-oven cookies.*

Ruskies

MAKES 7 DOZEN

A prizewinning recipe from the 2003 Doughmakers Baking Contest, submitted by Sandy Critchfield, Terre Haute, Indiana.

½ pound (2 sticks) butter, softened

One 8-ounce package cream cheese, softened

2 cups flour

½ box vanilla wafers, finely crushed

1 pound walnuts, finely crushed

1 8-ounce jar of pineapple preserves

Preheat the oven to 350°F.

Combine the butter and cream cheese. Mix in the flour to form a dough. Roll the dough out very thin and cut it with a diamond-shaped cookie cutter.

To make the filling, mix together the vanilla wafers, walnuts, and pineapple preserves. Place a teaspoon of the filling in the center of the cookie and roll up the sides, making sure to tuck in the loose edges. Bake for 15 minutes, or until golden brown.

▶ *One important step in getting good public relations for your company is to actually read the magazines or newspapers you want to write about you. Make note of the reporters' names that might cover your story. This way, when you pitch the story to them, you have a sense of the kind of story they like to write.*

Peanut Butter Cookies

MAKES 3 DOZEN

¾ cup peanut butter
½ cup solid vegetable
    shortening
1¼ cups firmly packed brown
    sugar
3 tablespoons milk

1 tablespoon vanilla extract
1 egg
1¾ cups flour
¾ teaspoon salt
¾ teaspoon baking soda

Preheat the oven to 350°F.

Combine the peanut butter, shortening, sugar, milk, and vanilla in a large bowl and beat until well blended. Add the egg and mix well. In a separate bowl, combine the flour, salt, and baking soda. Add the dry ingredients to the wet ones and mix until just blended.

Roll the dough into 1- to 2-inch balls (see Note). Place on a cookie sheet and flatten with the back of a fork so that the tines leave impressions on the tops of the cookies.

Bake for 7 minutes, or until lightly browned, and cool on a wire rack.

▶ *Mix the dough and shape the balls, then freeze them in zipper-sealed plastic bags. Keep a stash in the freezer that you can pull out when unexpected guests drop by or to make any ordinary occasion special.*

Pumpkin Cookies

MAKES ABOUT 4 DOZEN 2-OUNCE COOKIES

Submitted by Julie Young of Terre Haute, Indiana.

2 cups solid vegetable shortening

2 cups sugar

2 eggs

One 29-ounce can pumpkin

1 teaspoon vanilla extract

1½ teaspoons cinnamon

1 teaspoon salt

2 teaspoons baking soda

2 teaspoons baking powder

3 cups flour

ICING:

8 ounces cream cheese, softened

¼ pound (1 stick) butter, softened

3 cups confectioners' sugar

Preheat the oven to 375°F.

In the large bowl of an electric mixer, mix together the shortening and sugar on medium speed until well blended. Add the eggs, and when they are mixed in, add the pumpkin and vanilla. Continue mixing until well blended.

In a separate bowl, mix together the cinnamon, salt, baking soda, baking powder, and flour. Gradually add the flour mixture to the pumpkin mixture, about ½ cup at a time, mixing thoroughly after each addition.

Using a tablespoon or a 2-ounce cookie scoop, drop the batter on an ungreased cookie sheet, about 1 inch apart. Bake for 8 to 10 minutes, or until the cookies have domed and just barely begin to brown. Remove from the oven and allow to cool on a wire rack.

To make the icing: Combine the cream cheese and butter in the bowl of an electric mixer on medium speed. When these are well blended, gradually add the sugar until the icing is soft and easy to spread. Coat the cookies with the icing once they are completely cooled.

▶ *People like receiving care packages of cookies but not necessarily boxes of crumbs. So when sending cookies through the mail, use a sturdy box and wrap the cookies in groups of six to eight inside the larger carton to minimize breakage.*

Muffins

Blueberry Muffins

MAKES 12 MUFFINS, 24 MINI MUFFINS, OR 6 JUMBO MUFFINS

3 cups flour

2 cups sugar

¼ pound (1 stick) butter, softened, plus
    2 tablespoons

1 tablespoon baking powder

3 eggs

1 cup milk

1 cup blueberries

Preheat the oven to 350°F. Grease and flour muffin cups or use paper liners.

In a large bowl, blend the flour, sugar, stick of softened butter, and baking powder until crumbly. Set aside 1 cup. Add the eggs and milk to the remaining flour mixture and stir to combine. Gently fold in the blueberries. Pour the batter into the muffin cups, filling each about ⅔. Add the remaining 2 tablespoons of butter to the reserved topping and mix until crumbly. Sprinkle this on top of the muffins.

Bake for 15 to 18 minutes, until lightly browned.

▶ *When you must use frozen berries, toss the berries in a little cornstarch or flour before adding them to the muffin mix because frozen berries hold more moisture than fresh ones.*

Sweet Potato Muffins

MAKES 1 DOZEN

1 large orange-fleshed sweet
  potato (about 1¼
  pounds), baked until
  tender and peeled
2 eggs, beaten
½ cup milk
½ cup molasses
3 tablespoons butter, softened

1¼ cups all purpose flour
½ cup whole wheat flour
2 teaspoons baking powder
1 teaspoon cinnamon
¾ teaspoon salt
½ teaspoon ground ginger

Preheat the oven to 400°F. Grease a 12-cup regular muffin pan.

Cut the sweet potato into chunks and puree in a blender or food processor. Place 1 cup of puree in a large mixing bowl. Add the eggs, milk, molasses, and butter, and beat until completely blended. Add the flours, baking powder, cinnamon, salt, and ginger, and stir until just mixed.

Divide the batter among the muffin cups, filling each about ¾ full. Bake for 25 minutes, or until the tops are springy to the touch. Allow the pan to cool on a wire rack for 5 minutes, then turn out the muffins and allow to cool. Serve warm.

▶ *If your children are finicky eaters, get them to help you in the kitchen. They will be more likely to try foods they've helped prepare.*

Good Morning Muffins

MAKES 1 DOZEN

*I'll never forget how intimidated I felt at my first culinary professionals conference—a hairdresser surrounded by chefs and authors—but everyone was very nice and encouraging. In particular I remember how, toward the end of the exhibitors' time, a young lady came up and said she wanted to buy our display pans—all of them! Well, I loved that, but when she told me she was a test kitchen manager at Land O'Lakes, I was just blown away! Ever since then, Julie Ledvina has been a source of encouragement to us, and Land O'Lakes has generously supported us by allowing us to use their photos and recipes on our packaging. We are pleased to include some of their recipes in our book, especially this one. —*BETTE

½ cup firmly packed brown sugar

4 tablespoons LAND O LAKES® Butter, softened

1 cup LAND O LAKES® Sour Cream

2 LAND O LAKES® All Natural Farm Fresh Eggs

½ cup flaked coconut

½ cup raisins

2 medium carrots, shredded (about 1 cup)

1½ cups all purpose flour

1 teaspoon baking soda

1 teaspoon cinnamon

Preheat the oven to 375°F. Grease a 12-cup muffin pan thoroughly.

Combine the sugar and butter in a large mixing bowl and beat at medium speed, scraping the bowl often, until creamy, about 1 to 2 minutes. Add the sour cream and eggs, and continue beating until well mixed, another 1 to 2 minutes. Stir in the coconut, raisins, and carrots.

In a separate bowl, stir together the flour, baking soda, and cinnamon. Add to the sour cream mixture and stir just until moistened.

Spoon the batter into the muffin pan, filling each cup about ⅔ full. Bake for 20 to 25 minutes, or until lightly browned (see Tip).

▶ *For 6 jumbo muffins, bake for 28 to 32 minutes, or until lightly browned. For 32 mini muffins, bake for 15 to 18 minutes, or until lightly browned.*

Ready-to-Go Bran Muffins

MAKES UP TO 30 REGULAR-SIZE MUFFINS

2½ cups buttermilk

½ cup vegetable oil

2 eggs

3 cups crushed raisin–bran
  flake cereal

2½ cups flour

1 cup sugar

1¼ teaspoons baking powder

1 teaspoon baking soda

1 teaspoon salt

½ cup chopped nuts

In a large bowl, beat the buttermilk, oil, and eggs until well combined. Add the cereal, flour, sugar, baking powder, baking soda, salt, and nuts. Stir just until the dry ingredients are moistened. At this point the batter can be covered tightly and refrigerated for up to 2 weeks. You can scoop out enough batter to make the desired number of muffins.

When you are ready to bake, preheat the oven to 400°F. Grease the muffins cups and fill them halfway with the batter. Bake for 20 to 25 minutes, or until a tester inserted in the center comes out clean. (It will take longer for jumbo muffins and less time for mini muffins.) Remove the muffins immediately from the pan and serve.

▶ *When making muffins or quick breads, two cardinal rules are don't overmix and don't overbake. Gently mix the ingredients until just moistened and use a tester five minutes before the recipe says the bread should be done.*

Clementine's Muffins

MAKES 1 DOZEN

1½ cups all purpose flour

½ cup sugar

1½ teaspoons baking powder

½ teaspoon baking soda

½ teaspoon salt

⅓ cup orange juice

4 tablespoons butter, melted

1 egg

8 Clementine tangerines, peeled
 sectioned, and chopped (See Tip)

⅔ cup sweetened flaked coconut

1 tablespoon butter, softened

½ teaspoon grated orange zest

Preheat the oven to 375°F. Grease a 12-cup regular muffin pan.

Combine the flour, ¼ cup of sugar, baking powder, baking soda, and salt in a large bowl and mix well. In another bowl, mix together the orange juice, melted butter, and egg. Add this to the flour mixture and stir until the dry ingredients are just moistened. Fold the tangerine sections into the batter along with ⅓ cup of coconut. Spoon the batter into the prepared pan, filling each cup about ¾ full.

In a medium bowl, mix together the remaining ⅓ cup of coconut, ¼ cup of sugar, softened butter, and orange zest. Sprinkle evenly over the top of each muffin. Bake for 18 to 23 minutes, or until lightly browned.

Let the muffins cool in the pan for 5 minutes before removing.

▶ *You may substitute an 11-ounce can of mandarin oranges. Drain and chop the orange pieces.*

True Cornbread Muffins

MAKES 1 DOZEN

Here is a frontier recipe that we've adapted for our muffin pans using cornmeal and no flour. You'd think they would be heavy, but beating the egg whites lightens the muffins.

2 cups yellow cornmeal
½ teaspoon salt
3 teaspoons baking powder
2 cups milk
2 tablespoons butter
2 eggs, separated

Preheat the oven to 400°F. Grease 12 2½-inch muffin cups well.

In a medium bowl, mix together the cornmeal, salt, and baking powder. In a saucepan over medium-high heat, scald the milk. Remove from the heat, add the butter, and stir until the butter melts.

When the butter has melted, add the milk to the cornmeal mixture and stir to combine. Stir the egg yolks into the batter. In a separate bowl, beat the egg whites until soft peaks form, then fold them lightly into the batter. Spoon the batter into the prepared muffin cups, filling each cup ¾ full.

Bake for 30 minutes, until the tops begin to brown. Cool in the pan for 5 minutes before turning out. Serve warm and slathered with butter.

▶ *Dance like nobody is watching.*

A-B-C Muffins
(Apple-Banana-Cinnamon)

MAKES 2 DOZEN

2 cups all-purpose flour

1 teaspoon baking soda

1 teaspoon salt

½ teaspoon cinnamon

½ teaspoon nutmeg

⅔ cup solid vegetable shortening

1¼ cups sugar

2 eggs

1 teaspoon vanilla extract

¼ cup buttermilk

1 cup mashed ripe bananas

2 apples, peeled, cored, and shredded

Preheat the oven to 375°F. Grease and flour 24 muffin cups or use paper liners.

Sift together the flour, baking soda, salt, cinnamon, and nutmeg. In a large bowl, cream together the shortening and sugar until light and fluffy. Beat in the eggs, 1 at a time, then stir in the vanilla and buttermilk. Beat in the flour mixture just until incorporated. Fold in the mashed bananas and shredded apples. Fill each muffin cup half full.

Bake for 20 to 25 minutes, or until a toothpick inserted in the center comes out clean. Allow to cool.

▶ *Lasting brands are created by lots of public relations exposure, not with lots of advertising dollars. Ad dollars won't buy you a shortcut from the hard work of relentlessly pitching your product to editors and producers.*

Banana Raisin Oat Muffins

MAKES 1 DOZEN

1 egg, lightly beaten
1 cup milk
1 cup mashed ripe bananas (about 3 medium bananas)
½ cup granulated sugar
¼ cup vegetable oil
1 teaspoon vanilla

1 cup all-purpose flour or whole wheat flour
1 cup oat bran
⅔ cup raisins
1 teaspoon baking soda
1 teaspoon baking powder

Preheat oven to 400°F. Grease a 12-cup regular muffin pan.

In a large bowl, combine the egg, milk, bananas, sugar, oil, and vanilla and mix well.

In another bowl, mix together the flour, oat bran, raisins, baking soda, and baking powder. Stir the dry ingredients into the egg mixture until just combined.

Divide batter among muffin cups, filling each one about ¾ full. Bake for 20 to 25 minutes or until tops are firm to the touch.

▶ *For a flavorful adventure, you may substitute dried cranberries, cherries, or chopped figs for the raisins.*

Apple Butter Muffins

MAKES 1 DOZEN

Here is a moist and delicious breakfast muffin that uses natural sweeteners and a minimal amount of fat.

1 cup natural apple butter	1 cup all-purpose flour
1 egg	2 teaspoons baking powder
2 tablespoons oil	¾ teaspoon baking soda
¼ cup honey	½ teaspoon cinnamon
1 cup whole wheat flour	¼ teaspoon nutmeg

Preheat the oven to 375°F. Grease a 12-cup regular muffin pan.

In a large bowl, beat together the apple butter, egg, oil, and honey. In a medium bowl, combine the flours, baking powder, baking soda, cinnamon, and nutmeg. Add the dry ingredients to the wet ones and stir until just moistened.

Fill each muffin cup about ¾ full. Bake for 20 minutes, until the tops are firm or a tester inserted in the center comes out clean.

▶ *To make it easier to remove honey, molasses, or syrup from a measuring cup, try spraying it with nonstick cooking spray before adding the sticky ingredient.*

Blackberry Muffins

MAKES 1 DOZEN

1 cup all-purpose flour, plus
    ¼ cup if using frozen berries
¾ cup cornmeal
1 tablespoon brown sugar
2 teaspoons baking powder
½ teaspoon salt

¼ teaspoon baking soda
¾ cup milk
4 tablespoons butter, melted
1 egg
1 cup blackberries, fresh or frozen

Preheat the oven to 425°. Grease a 12-cup regular muffin pan.

In a large bowl, combine 1 cup of flour, cornmeal, sugar, baking powder, salt, and baking soda. In a medium bowl, whisk together the milk, butter, and egg. Stir the wet ingredients into the dry ones until just moistened.

If using frozen berries, thaw and dry them, toss with the ¼ cup of flour, and fold them into the batter. If using fresh berries, wash and dry them, and fold them into the batter.

Fill the muffin cups ¾ full. Bake for 15 to 20 minutes, or until the tops are golden brown. Allow to cool for 5 minutes in the pan and then serve warm.

▶ *Brown sugar that has become hard can be softened by using a Brown Sugar Bear or similar product. These are terra-cotta disks that you soak in water, pat dry, and then add to the container where you store your brown sugar. They are reasonably priced and really work!*

Café au Lait Muffins

MAKES 1 DOZEN

2 cups all-purpose flour

½ cup sugar

2½ teaspoons baking powder

½ teaspoon salt

½ teaspoon cinnamon

1 cup milk

¼ pound (1 stick) butter

1 egg, beaten

1 teaspoon vanilla extract

1 tablespoon instant coffee
   granules

¾ cup semisweet chocolate chips

Preheat the oven to 375°F. Grease a 12-cup regular muffin pan.

In a large bowl, whisk together the flour, sugar, baking powder, salt, and cinnamon. In a heavy saucepan over medium-high heat, scald the milk, then remove the pan from the heat. Add the butter to the milk and stir until the butter melts. Add the egg, vanilla, and instant coffee to the milk mixture. Whisk until well combined and the coffee granules have dissolved. Add to the flour mixture and stir until the dry ingredients are just moistened. Fold the chocolate chips into the batter.

Spoon the batter into the muffin cups, filling them about ¾ full. Bake for 15 to 20 minutes, or until the tops are lightly browned.

▶ *Early on, we had baseball caps made with this embroidered motto: "Live well. Laugh often. Love much." In the busiest seasons it is hard to remember these rules to live by, so it's a good thing we wrote them down.*

Lemon Tea Muffins

MAKES 1 DOZEN

2 eggs, separated
¼ pound (1 stick) butter, softened
½ cup plus 1 tablespoon sugar

1 cup flour
1 teaspoon baking powder
¼ teaspoon salt
3 tablespoons lemon juice
⅛ teaspoon cinnamon

Preheat the oven to 350°F. Grease a 12-cup regular muffin pan.

In a small bowl, beat the egg yolks until light and lemon-colored, about 3 minutes. In a large bowl, cream together the butter and ½ cup of sugar. Fold the yolks into the butter-sugar mixture. In another large bowl, whisk together the flour, baking powder, and salt. Add to the butter-sugar mixture and stir until just combined. Add the lemon juice and stir until blended. In a separate bowl, beat the egg whites until soft peaks form and fold them into the batter.

Spoon the batter into the muffin cups, filling them ¾ full. In a small bowl, mix together the remaining 1 tablespoon of sugar and the cinnamon, and sprinkle it over the muffin batter.

Bake for 20 to 25 minutes, or until the tops are firm and a tester inserted in the center comes out clean.

▶ *Cold eggs separate more easily than room temperature ones.*

Porter Peach Muffins

MAKES 1 DOZEN

We go to Oklahoma several times a year to do shows such as the Affair of the Heart in Oklahoma City and Heart of Tulsa because the people there are so good to us and really like our bakeware. We first made this recipe with peaches from Porter, Oklahoma, a town said to have some of the best peaches in the country. If you travel on I-40, look for them.

1½ cups flour

1 cup sugar

¾ teaspoon salt

½ teaspoon baking soda

2 eggs

½ cup vegetable oil

½ teaspoon vanilla extract

⅛ teaspoon almond extract

1¼ cups peeled and chopped fresh peaches

½ cup chopped almonds

Preheat the oven to 375°F. Grease a 12-cup regular muffin pan.

In a large bowl, whisk together the flour, sugar, salt, and baking soda. In a medium bowl, combine the eggs, oil, and vanilla and almond extracts. Add the dry ingredients to the wet ones and stir until the dry ingredients are just moistened. Fold the peaches and almonds into the batter. Spoon the batter into the muffin cups until ¾ full.

Bake for 20 to 25 minutes, until the tops begin to brown.

▶ *February is Bake for Family Fun Month. Get ideas for baking together at the Home Baking Association website, www.homebaking.org.*

Spicy Cheese Muffins

MAKES 1 DOZEN

This is a great muffin to serve with chili.

2½ cups all-purpose flour

¼ cup yellow cornmeal

¼ cup sugar

2 tablespoons baking powder

½ teaspoon salt

¼ teaspoon cayenne pepper, or more to taste

⅛ teaspoon black pepper, or more to taste

¾ cup finely grated cheddar cheese (about 3 ounces)

2 tablespoons finely chopped onion

1 tablespoon finely chopped green bell pepper

One 2-ounce jar diced pimiento

2 eggs, beaten

1½ cups milk

¼ cup vegetable oil

Preheat the oven to 400°F. Grease a 12-cup regular muffin pan.

In a large bowl, whisk together the flour, cornmeal, sugar, baking powder, salt, cayenne, and black pepper until evenly blended. Add the cheese, onion, and green pepper, and stir until evenly mixed. In a separate bowl, whisk together the eggs, milk, and oil. Add these to the dry ingredients and stir until just moistened. Spoon the batter into the muffin cups until about ¾ full.

Bake for 20 to 25 minutes, until lightly browned on top. Remove from the pans immediately and serve while hot.

▶ *Invest in a good oven thermometer and use it! Ovens vary in how accurately they keep temperature, and over time your oven's thermostat can become inaccurate.*

Dreaming of New England Muffins

MAKES 1 DOZEN

The maple flavor in these muffins makes us think of changing leaves, quaint town squares, and, of course, the eighteen-day, twelve hour-a-day, five-state New England fair known as the Eastern States Exposition, or simply The Big E. The twenty six-hour drive each way crowns the experience as the most exhausting show we've ever done.

2 cups all-purpose flour
½ cup packed brown sugar
2 teaspoons baking powder
½ teaspoon salt
¾ cup milk
¼ pound (1 stick) butter or
    margarine, melted
½ cup maple syrup
¼ cup sour cream

1 egg
½ teaspoon vanilla extract

TOPPING:
3 tablespoons flour
2 tablespoons chopped nuts
3 tablespoons sugar
½ teaspoon cinnamon
2 tablespoons cold butter, cut into
    chunks

Preheat the oven to 400°F. Grease a 12-cup regular muffin pan.

In a large bowl, combine the flour, brown sugar, baking powder, and salt. In another bowl, combine the milk, butter, syrup, sour cream, egg, and vanilla. Stir the wet ingredients into the dry ones and mix until the dry ingredients are just moistened. Spoon the batter into the muffin cups until ¾ full.

To make the topping: Combine the flour, nuts, sugar, and cinnamon in a medium bowl. Cut in the butter until the mixture resembles coarse crumbs. Sprinkle over the batter and bake for 16 to 20 minutes, or until a tester inserted in the center comes out clean.

Cool in the pan for 5 minutes on a wire rack before removing and serve while still warm.

▶ *Most baking ingredient manufacturers have websites with a wealth of information about what you can do with their products. Many will answer your email questions. These are great resources for learning more.*

Pastry and Pies

Perfect Piecrust

MAKES ONE DOUBLE-CRUST PIE

2 cups sifted flour
1 teaspoon salt
⅔ cup solid vegetable shortening or cold butter,
    or a combination of the two
4 to 6 tablespoons ice water

In a large bowl, stir the flour and salt together with a fork. Cut in the shortening with a pastry blender until crumbly. Stir in the ice water with a fork, little by little, until the dough holds together. Use your fingertips to form the dough into 2 balls of equal size for 2 open-faced pies. If making a double-crust pie, 1 ball should be slightly larger than the other since the bottom crust requires a little more dough.

Cover the dough balls with plastic wrap and chill for at least 30 minutes. They may be kept for a few days in the refrigerator or stored for up to 2 months in the freezer. If frozen, allow to thaw before rolling out.

Roll the chilled dough out evenly on a lightly floured pastry cloth to the desired size, usually the diameter of the pan plus ½ inch all around so you can crimp or flute the edge.

VARIATION

If you have a food processor, here is a quick and easy way to get your pie pastry started. Measure the flour, salt, and shortening into the bowl of a food processor fitted with a metal blade. Pulse the blade until the mixture inside is crumbly. Turn the processor on and immediately begin to drizzle the cold water into the bowl. The dough should catch up into a loose ball about the time all the water is added. Turn off the food processor. Place the ball of dough on a work surface and form it into two balls, then wrap and chill.

Too much warmth or overworking the dough will speed the formation of gluten and make your crust chewy rather than flaky or crumbly. Therefore, handle the dough as little as possible and try to use your fingertips rather than your palms. Make sure the ice water is really cold. Don't skip the step of chilling the dough.

Baking the Pie Shell

If a pie filling recipe calls for prebaking the piecrust, line the pastry with heavy foil and bake it at 400°F for 8 minutes, then remove the foil and bake 3 to 5 minutes more, until the crust is lightly golden.

If you fear your piecrust will fall apart when you transfer it to the pie pan, try one of these two tricks:

1. Place the pie pan facedown on top of the dough. Slide one hand under the pastry cloth and put the other on the bottom of the pan. In a quick motion, invert the pan and then peel away the cloth.

2. After rolling out the pie pastry, start at one edge of the pastry to loosely roll it back onto the rolling pin so that the pastry is wrapped around the pin. Move the pin with the pastry to the edge of the pie pan and unroll it into place.

▶ *If you wish, you can cut shapes out of the dough, such as with a small heart-shaped cookie cutter. You can then lay the cut-out heart shapes on top of the top crust for additional decoration. Or you can use a paring knife to cut your own pattern into the top crust.*

Sour Cream Pie Pastry

MAKES ENOUGH FOR 1 DOUBLE-CRUST 9-INCH PIE OR 2 SINGLE-CRUST 9-INCH PIES

Sour cream provides just the right touch of acidity, inhibits toughness, and lends its lovely flavor and dairy goodness. Use this pastry with any pie filling.

¼ pound (2 sticks) cold butter, cut into small chunks
½ cup solid vegetable shortening
2½ cups all purpose flour

2 to 4 tablespoons ice water
¾ teaspoon salt
1 teaspoon sugar
6 tablespoons sour cream

In a large bowl, blend the butter and shortening into the flour using your fingers; the mixture will be crumbly, not smooth. In a small bowl, stir together 2 tablespoons of water, the salt, and sugar. Add the sour cream and stir well.

Make a well in the center of the flour mixture and stir in the sour cream mixture. Mix lightly with a fork to combine. Knead the dough very gently into a soft mass.

Turn the dough out onto a lightly floured board and pat it into a flattened disk. Cover it with plastic wrap and refrigerate for at least 1 hour or up to 3 days before using. The pastry may also be frozen for up to 4 months.

If the pie recipe calls for prebaked pastry, bake it at 400°F for 15 to 17 minutes.

▶ *Pay attention to the smallest details of your business and take pride in them. Encourage your employees to do the same. Brian Critchfield, who runs our shipping department, has received handwritten notes from retailers thanking him for the nice job he does packing the product for shipping. In contrast, we've received products wrapped in shredded newspaper. People will notice the difference.*

Clabber Girl
Hot Water Piecrust

MAKES ENOUGH PASTRY FOR 1 DOUBLE-CRUST 9-INCH PIE

This recipe first appeared in the 1937 Clabber Girl Baking Book, *and it is very different from the piecrust recipes you see today. Try it when you are looking for something special with your favorite pie filling.* —BETTE

¼ cup boiling water
½ cup solid vegetable shortening
1½ cups all purpose flour, sifted
½ teaspoon Clabber Girl Baking Powder
½ teaspoon salt

In a small mixing bowl, pour the boiling water over the shortening and beat until creamy. Sift in the flour, baking powder, and salt, and stir until the dough holds together. Turn the dough out onto a work surface and form it into 2 balls. Cover them with plastic wrap and chill about 2 hours. Roll each dough ball out to a ⅛ inch thickness. Transfer the pastry to a pie pan.

If your recipe calls for a prebaked pie pastry, bake it at 450°F for 15 minutes, or until lightly browned.

▶ *Keep a journal of the problems you face, and be sure to write down the solutions when you find them, too. When you get discouraged, look back on how much you've accomplished, and you'll find the strength to meet the challenge at hand.*

Apple Raspberry Pie

MAKES ONE 9-INCH PIE

1 recipe Perfect Piecrust, for a
double-crust pie (page 217)

4½ cups peeled and sliced (¼ inch)
apples

2 cups raspberries, fresh or frozen

1 tablespoon lemon juice

⅔ cup plus 1 tablespoon sugar

3 tablespoons cornstarch

½ teaspoon almond extract

1 egg beaten with 1 tablespoon cold
water

1 cup heavy cream

Prepare the piecrust as directed, setting aside the smaller ball of dough.

In a large bowl, toss the apples and raspberries with the lemon juice. Add ⅔ cup of sugar, the cornstarch, and almond extract. Toss to coat all the ingredients.

Roll out the larger ball of dough on a floured surface and transfer it to the pie pan. Don't trim any excess pastry from the edge yet. Place the apples and raspberries in the prepared crust and sprinkle the remaining sugar on top. Leave room at the edges for sealing and crimping the top crust.

Roll out the smaller ball of dough on a lightly floured board into a 9-inch circle, about ⅛ inch thick. Create a few small openings for the heat to vent from the top crust. Lay the crust over the pie filling and seal by fluting or pinching the edges. Chill in the refrigerator for 30 minutes before baking.

Preheat the oven to 400°F. Bake for 10 minutes, then lower the temperature to 350°F. Brush top crust with egg-water mixture. Bake for 50 to 60 minutes, until the crust is golden and the filling is bubbling in the center. (You can place a one-piece crust protector on the pie about halfway through baking to prevent the rim of the crust from becoming overdone.)

Remove from the oven and pour the cream through the openings in no more than 4 spots because the cream will spread throughout the pie. Allow the pie to cool slightly to make it easier to cut and serve, and serve while it is still a little warm. Store any unfinished pie in the refrigerator, covered with plastic wrap, for up to 3 days. Bring to room temperature before serving.

► *You may find it necessary to hire outside professionals to assist you, such as ad agencies, sales consultants, and product designers. They can be valuable, but never give up your opinion or let them lead you in a direction that runs counter to your instinct or vision. This is your company, your dream. No one has ownership of it the way you do.*

Chocolate Pecan Pie

MAKES ONE 9-INCH PIE

Offered by Nancy Wagnon of Birmingham, Alabama.

½ recipe Perfect Piecrust (page 217),
   prebaked for an open-faced pie

2 cups sugar

4 heaping tablespoons unsweetened
   cocoa

4 eggs

½ cup buttermilk

1 teaspoon vanilla extract

¼ pound (1 stick) butter, melted

1 cup chopped pecans, plus
   6 pecan halves

Preheat the oven to 400°F.

Prepare the piecrust as directed.

In a bowl, whisk together the sugar and cocoa until blended. In a separate bowl, whisk together the eggs, buttermilk, and vanilla. Add to the sugar cocoa mixture and stir until combined. Gently stir in the melted butter and 1 cup of pecans. Place this filling in the prebaked pie shell and spread with a spoon or spatula until evenly distributed. Place the pecan halves on top of the filling, arranged in a circle to indicate slices or in some other design.

Bake for 10 minutes, then lower the temperature to 300°F and bake until the filling is firm, about 45 minutes. Add a piecrust protector after the first 10 minutes at 300°F to prevent the crust from overbaking.

▶ *Don't use aluminum foil to protect your piecrusts. Get the Doughmakers Pie Pan with Crust Protector set. It'll change the way you think about baking pies!*

Classic Coconut Cream Pie

MAKES 1 AWESOME 9-INCH PIE

This pie recipe, offered by Julie Young of Terre Haute, Indiana, was the Grand Champion winner in the 2003 Doughmakers Baking Contest. Julie graciously offered to help us test and edit the recipes in this book—and taught us a thing or two about baking in the process. Thanks, Julie!

CRUST:
3 cups flour
1 teaspoon salt
1¼ cups solid vegetable shortening
1 egg
¼ cup water
1 tablespoon vinegar

FILLING:
2 cups sugar
⅔ cup cornstarch
6 egg yolks

5 cups milk
½ cup shredded coconut, plus additional for sprinkling
1 tablespoon vanilla extract
4 tablespoons butter

MERINGUE:
8 egg whites
¾ cup sugar
Pinch of salt
⅓ cup white Karo syrup

Preheat the oven to 350°F.

To make the crust: Mix the flour and salt, then cut in the shortening until crumbly. In a separate bowl, whisk together the egg, water, and vinegar. Add to the flour mixture and stir until the dough begins to hold together. Form the dough into a flattened disk and roll it out to fit a 9-inch pie pan. Bake for 15 to 20 minutes, or until golden brown. Allow the crust to cool in the pan on a wire rack.

To make the filling: In a heavy saucepan over medium heat, mix the sugar, cornstarch, and egg yolks. Slowly add the milk and continue to cook over medium heat until thick, about 7 minutes. Remove from the heat and stir in the coconut, vanilla, and butter. Pour this filling into the cooled pie shell.

To make the meringue: Beat the egg whites till frothy. Add the sugar slowly and beat until almost stiff. Add the salt and syrup, and beat until soft peaks form. Spoon on top of the pie filling and sprinkle with additional coconut. Place in a 350°F oven until the meringue turns lightly brown, about 5 minutes.

▶ *Reluctant customers will always challenge the price of your product. Always bring the conversation back to the quality, the features, and the benefits.*

Christmas Clafoutis

MAKES 6 TO 8 SERVINGS

I developed this variation of a rustic French dessert for a cooking class I gave right after we introduced our pie pan. The pastry helps give shape and texture to this fruit flan. The colors and flavors make this lighter dessert work well in the Christmas season. —BETTE

½ recipe Perfect Piecrust (page 217), prebaked for an open-faced pie

CLAFOUTIS:
¾ cup milk
1 large egg, at room temperature
1 large egg yolk, at room temperature
2 tablespoons framboise (raspberry brandy)
½ cup sugar

¾ cup plus 1 tablespoon all-purpose flour
¼ pound (1 stick) plus 2 tablespoons butter, softened
2 cups raspberries

SAUCE:
1 cup raspberries
½ cup orange juice
½ cup sugar
1 tablespoon framboise

Preheat the oven to 400°F.

Prepare the piecrust as directed.

To make the clafoutis: Combine the milk, egg, egg yolk, framboise, sugar, flour, and butter in a blender or food processor. Pour into the prepared pie pan. Scatter the raspberries over the batter in a single layer. Bake until the top of the clafoutis is puffed up, lightly browned on top, and set, about 38 to 45 minutes.

To make the sauce: In a heavy saucepan over medium heat, heat the raspberries, orange juice, sugar, and framboise, stirring constantly, until it begins to thicken, about 15 minutes. Cool the sauce until it is warm. Transfer the ingredients to a blender and puree. Serve the warm sauce over the clafoutis at room temperature.

▶ *A quick way to clean your blender is to put a cup of hot water and a little soap in the jar and turn it on for 30 seconds to a minute. This will help loosen dried-on foods.*

Grandma's Touch Apple Pie with Creamy Caramel Sauce

MAKES ONE 9-INCH PIE

½ recipe Perfect Piecrust (page 217), prebaked for an open-faced pie

8 medium Granny Smith apples

½ cup sugar

¾ cup flour

5⅓ tablespoons chilled butter

½ cup chopped pecan pieces, toasted

CREAMY CARAMEL SAUCE:

¾ cup sugar

¼ cup water

6 tablespoons light corn syrup

Pinch of salt

½ cup heavy cream

½ teaspoon vanilla extract

Preheat the oven to 450°F.

Prepare the piecrust as directed.

Cut the apples into slices and layer them in the bottom crust. In a large bowl, mix the sugar with the flour, then cut in the butter until the mixture becomes crumbly. Stir in the pecans. Sprinkle this crumb mixture over the apples.

Bake for 10 minutes, then lower the temperature to 350°F for 40 minutes. Pierce the apples with a fork to check for tenderness; they are done when they give only slight resistance.

While the pie is baking, prepare the sauce: In a heavy saucepan over medium-low heat, simmer the sugar, water, corn syrup, and salt, stirring, until the sugar is dissolved. Bring the mixture to a low boil, without stirring, until it is a golden caramel color, about 3 to 5 minutes. Remove the pan from the heat and add the cream and vanilla, stirring until well combined, about 1 minute. Cool the sauce to room temperature. The sauce will thicken as it cools. (Makes about ¾ cup of caramel sauce.)

Cut the pie into slices and serve warm with vanilla ice cream. Drizzle the Creamy Caramel Sauce over the pie and ice cream.

▶ *When calling an editor or producer about doing a feature story on your company, the approach has to be that you are trying to make their job easier: You're offering a great story, you'll set up the interviews, you'll deliver the pictures—whatever it takes. Nothing turns off an editor faster than the attitude that you deserve their attention or that they should give you exposure.*

Jamberry Pie

MAKES ONE 9-INCH PIE

When my daughter Gracie was born, my sister gave us a children's book by Bruce Degan called Jam-berry, which is a wonderful, whimsical adventure of a little boy and a berry-picking bear. I used to love reading this book to Gracie at bedtime. Then I put together this berry pie so we could have Jamberry all day long! —WILLIAM WAGNON

1 recipe Perfect Piecrust
    (page 217), bottom crust
    prebaked
3 tablespoons cornstarch
¼ cup water

⅔ cup sugar
½ pint blackberries
½ pint raspberries
½ pint blueberries
¼ teaspoon cinnamon

Preheat the oven to 450°F.

Prepare the piecrust as directed.

In a mixing bowl, whisk the cornstarch into the water until dissolved. Add the sugar and whisk until smoothly blended. Wash the berries and then gently fold them into the sugar mix-ture until well coated. Sprinkle with the cinnamon.

Arrange the berries on the piecrust in a deep dish pie pan. Drizzle with any sugar mixture that might be left over. Cover with the top crust, making a few holes in it to allow steam to vent.

Bake for 10 minutes, then lower the temperature to 350°F. Bake 40 minutes more, or until the crust is well browned. Allow the pie to cool before slicing.

▶ *When thickening fruits for pies, mix the cornstarch and sugar together first. The sugar will help break down lumps in the cornstarch before it is added to the fruit.*

Lemon Chess Pie

MAKES ONE 9-INCH PIE

Offered by Nancy Wagnon, Birmingham, Alabama.

½ recipe Perfect Piecrust (page 217), prebaked for an open-faced pie

1½ cups granulated sugar

4 eggs

2 teaspoons white vinegar

12 tablespoons (1½ sticks) butter, melted

3 teaspoons white cornmeal

Dash of salt

2 teaspoons vanilla extract

5 tablespoons freshly squeezed lemon juice

Confectioners' sugar

Preheat the oven to 350°F.

Prepare the piecrust as directed.

In a large bowl, combine the granulated sugar and eggs. Add the vinegar, butter, cornmeal, and salt, stirring to combine. Add the vanilla and lemon juice, and stir until well blended.

Pour the filling into the piecrust and bake for 30 minutes, or until firm. Allow to cool, then dust with confectioners' sugar. Slice this pie thinly because it is very rich.

▶ *Reduce clean-up time when using a food processor: Cover the bowl with plastic wrap before putting the lid on. This will keep food out of the lid and chute, which are the toughest parts to clean.*

Lemon Chiffon Pie

MAKES ONE 9-INCH PIE

½ recipe Perfect Piecrust (page 217), prebaked for an open-faced pie

4 eggs, separated

½ scant teaspoon salt

1 cup plus 1½ teaspoons sugar

½ cup lemon juice

1 teaspoon grated lemon rind

¾ tablespoon unflavored gelatin

¼ cup cold water

¾ cup heavy cream

½ teaspoon vanilla extract

Beat the egg yolks and salt in the top of a double boiler. Turn the heat to medium-high and gradually add ½ cup of sugar. Add the lemon juice and rind, and cook until a custard forms, about 10 minutes. Remove from the heat.

In a small bowl, soften the gelatin in the cold water. Add it to the hot custard and stir until completely dissolved. Chill the custard in the refrigerator until cool.

In a medium bowl, beat the egg whites until stiff. Add ½ cup of sugar and beat until soft peaks form. When the custard is beginning to congeal, fold in the stiffly beaten egg whites. Pour the custard into a deep 9-inch baked pie shell and chill in the refrigerator for at least 1 hour.

Whip the cream with the remaining 1½ teaspoons of sugar and the vanilla, and spread it over the custard before serving.

▶ *Be a local hero. Even if your company serves a national market, make an effort to contribute to local causes and give time to your community. The people in your hometown will become your cheerleaders and ambassadors.*

Lemon Meringue Pie

MAKES ONE 9-INCH PIE

½ recipe Perfect Piecrust (page 217),
  prebaked for an open-faced pie

2 cups water

1½ cups sugar

½ cup cornstarch

5 eggs, separated

4 tablespoons butter

¾ cup fresh lemon juice

1 tablespoon grated lemon zest

1½ teaspoons vanilla extract

¼ teaspoon cream of tartar

¼ teaspoon salt

Preheat the oven to 375°F.

Prepare the piecrust as directed.

Bring the water to a boil in a heavy saucepan. Remove from the heat and let cool for 5 minutes. In a small bowl, whisk together the 1 cup of sugar and the cornstarch. Add to the hot water, stirring until completely blended. Return the saucepan to medium-high heat, stirring constantly until the mixture comes to a boil. Scoop about ½ cup of liquid from the saucepan and beat with the egg yolks until smooth. Add back to the saucepan and beat until smooth. Bring to another boil over medium-high heat. Remove from the heat and add the butter, stirring until just dissolved. Add the lemon juice, zest, and 1 teaspoon of vanilla, and stir until combined. Pour into the prepared crust. Cover with plastic wrap to prevent a skin from forming while you prepare the meringue.

With an electric hand mixer, beat the egg whites with the cream of tartar, salt, and remaining ½ teaspoon of vanilla until soft peaks form. Add the ½ cup sugar gradually while continuing to beat to stiff peaks. Remove the plastic wrap from the custard and pile this meringue on top, making sure to spread it all the way to the crust of the pie to seal the custard. Bake for 15 to 20 minutes, until golden edges appear on the meringue folds. Cool the pie on a wire rack.

▶ *If you are separating a lot of eggs, you can crack all the eggs into a bowl and then scoop out the yolks with your fingers. If you chill the eggs first, the yolks will be less likely to break when using this technique.*

Peach Pie

MAKES ONE 9-INCH DOUBLE-CRUST PIE

A prizewinning recipe from the 2003 Doughmakers Baking Contest, submitted by Virginia Oard, Terre Haute, Indiana.

2 cups plus 3 tablespoons all-purpose flour

Salt

⅔ cup solid vegetable shortening

6 to 7 tablespoons cold water

2 large cans (1 pound 13 ounces each) sliced peaches

1 teaspoon lemon juice

1 scant teaspoon almond extract

¾ cup plus 1 teaspoon sugar

3 tablespoons butter

1 tablespoon milk

To make the crust: sift together 2 cups of flour and ½ teaspoon of salt in a large bowl. Cut in the shortening with a fork or pastry blender. Stir in the water gradually with a fork until you can form the dough into a ball. Divide the dough into 2 slightly uneven balls and chill them in the refrigerator for 30 minutes. Roll out the larger ball on a floured pastry cloth to fit a 9-inch pie pan.

Preheat the oven to 400°F.

Drain the peaches, reserving ½ cup of the syrup. Mix together the syrup, lemon juice, and almond extract. Add to the peaches and toss to coat. Combine the remaining 3 tablespoons of flour, ¾ cup of sugar, and a dash of salt, add to the peaches and toss to coat. Fill the pie shell with this mixture and dot with the butter. Roll out the top crust and place it over the pie filling, sealing the top crust to the bottom crust and decorating the rim as desired. Brush the top of the pie with the milk and sprinkle the remaining 1 teaspoon of sugar over the top. Bake for 40 to 45 minutes, until the filling is bubbly and the crust is browned. Cool the pie on a wire rack before slicing.

▶ *If your cutting board slides around, place a damp paper towel beneath it before you begin chopping. The paper towel can then be used to wipe the counter when you are done.*

Pecan Caramel Silk Pie

MAKES 12 SERVINGS

This recipe is pictured on the packaging of our 9-inch pie pan with crust protector. Our thanks to Land O'Lakes for this and all the photos they contributed to our retail packaging!

CRUST:

1 cup graham cracker crumbs

¼ cup finely chopped pecans

¼ cup LAND O LAKES® Butter, melted

2 tablespoons sugar

FILLING:

¾ cup LAND O LAKES® Butter, softened

1 cup sugar

Two 1-ounce squares unsweetened baking chocolate, melted and cooled

2 teaspoons vanilla extract

½ cup pasteurized refrigerated egg substitute

TOPPING:

1 cup chilled heavy cream

1 tablespoon thick caramel ice cream topping, warmed

1 tablespoon thick chocolate ice cream topping, warmed

12 pecan halves

Preheat the oven to 350°F.

In a small bowl, stir together all the crust ingredients. Press the crumbs into a 9-inch pie pan. Bake for 8 to 10 minutes, or until lightly browned. Set the pan on a wire rack to cool completely.

To make the filling; Put the butter and sugar in the large bowl of an electric mixer. Beat at medium speed, scraping the bowl often, until creamy, about 3 minutes. Stir in the chocolate and vanilla. Add ¼ cup of the egg substitute and continue beating for 5 minutes. Add the remaining egg substitute and beat for another 5 minutes. Spoon the mixture into the crust and refrigerate until firm, about 4 hours or overnight.

At serving time, beat the heavy cream in a medium mixing bowl at high speed, scraping the bowl often, until stiff peaks form, about 3 minutes. Cut the pie into 12 slices and transfer to serving plates. Place a dollop of cream on each serving or use a piping bag for a more elaborate decoration. Drizzle each serving with caramel topping and chocolate topping. Garnish with a pecan half.

▶ *Not only is aluminum bakeware very efficient at heating up to give you better baking, but it also sheds heat quickly when removed from the oven. This means recipes that call for cooling foods in the pan, such as this one, are ready more quickly. It also means that foods won't continue cooking long after you take them out of the oven, which can happen if a pan holds the heat too long.*

Classic Pumpkin Pie

MAKES TWO 9-INCH PIES

One pumpkin pie is never enough. This recipe will set you up with two delicious pies for that holiday dinner.

CRUST:

2 cups all-purpose flour

¼ teaspoon salt

⅓ pound (10⅔ tablespoons) cold butter, cut into chunks

4 to 5 tablespoons cold water

FILLING:

4 eggs

1½ cups firmly packed brown sugar

One 12-ounce can evaporated milk

1 29-ounce can pumpkin pie filling

2 teaspoons cinnamon

1 teaspoon ground ginger

½ teaspoon cloves

1 teaspoon salt

GINGER WHIPPED CREAM:

1 cup chilled heavy cream

2 tablespoons sugar

½ teaspoon ground ginger

To make the piecrust: Place the flour and salt in the bowl of a food processor fitted with a metal blade and pulse briefly to mix. Add the butter and pulse until the mixture resembles coarse crumbs. Add water, 1 tablespoon at a time, and pulse for 10 seconds after each addition. When the dough begins to hold together, stop adding water. Turn the dough out onto a work surface and shape into 2 balls. Flatten the balls into disks or mounds, then wrap and chill in the refrigerator for about 20 minutes.

Preheat the oven to 425°F.

To make the filling: Beat the eggs in a large mixing bowl at medium speed until thick and lemon-colored, about 2 minutes. Add the sugar, milk, pie filling, cinnamon, ginger, cloves, and salt. Beat until well mixed, about another 2 minutes.

On a lightly floured surface, roll out 1 ball of dough into a 12-inch circle. Fold it into quarters and place in a 9-inch pie pan. Unfold, pressing firmly against the bottom and sides. Trim the crust to ½ inch from the edge of the pan. Crimp or flute the edge. Repeat with the other ball of dough.

Pour half of the filling ingredients into each crust and bake for 10 minutes. Lower the oven temperature to 350°F and continue baking for 40 to 50 minutes, or until a knife inserted in the center comes out clean. When the rim of the crust reaches the desired shade of brown, place a one-piece pie crust protector over the pie to prevent of the crust from burning. Cool completely after baking.

To make the topping: In a small chilled mixing bowl, beat the cream at high speed, scraping the bowl often, until soft peaks form, about 8 to 10 minutes. Add the sugar and ginger, and continue beating until stiff peaks form, another 1 to 2 minutes.

▶ *Life is too short not to enjoy your work. So if you have a dream, follow it.*

Pizza

Long-Rise Pizza Dough

MAKES 2 THICK 15-INCH PIZZAS OR 3 THIN 12-INCH PIZZAS

This is my family's favorite recipe, refined over ten years of family pizza nights. It doesn't take any more time than any other pizza dough, you just start in the morning and let it rise until dinner time. The great flavor comes from starting with a sponge and the long rising time.

—WILLIAM WAGNON, Doughmakers Vice President of Marketing

SPONGE:

¼ cup warm water

1 tablespoon quick rise or one ¼-ounce package active dry yeast

¼ cup bread flour

DOUGH:

1¾ cups warm water

3 tablespoons olive oil

1 teaspoon kosher salt

4¾ to 5¾ cups bread flour

Toppings of your choice

Olive oil for pans

Combine the sponge ingredients in a large mixing bowl and allow to sit for 10 to 15 minutes or longer. The longer the sponge has to work, the more flavor there will be in the crust.

To make the dough: Add the water to the sponge and stir with a whisk until the sponge dissolves. Add 1 tablespoon of oil and stir to blend. Add the salt and stir until it dissolves.

Add the flour, 1 cup at a time, mixing well after each addition, until 4¾ cups have been added. Turn the dough out onto a work surface and begin to knead, mixing in any loose bits of flour or dough. If the dough is too sticky to work with your hands, add a little more flour but no more than necessary.

Knead the dough until it is smooth and elastic, and shape it into a ball. Clean the mixing bowl and add the remaining 2 teaspoons of oil. Return the dough to the bowl and turn it until it is coated with oil. Cover with plastic wrap or a damp towel and let rise in a warm place for 5 to 8 hours, punching it down halfway through.

Preheat the oven to 500°F.

Punch the dough down and turn it out onto a work surface that is lightly floured if necessary. Divide the dough into halves—or thirds if you like thinner pizza—and shape each portion into a domed disk. Cover the dough with a dish towel and allow to rest while you prepare the toppings, about 10 minutes. (Alternatively, after this resting period you can cover the dough tightly in plastic wrap and freeze it. Remove from the freezer at least 45 minutes before using.)

Shape the pizza dough with your hands and fingertips. Do not use a rolling pin.

Add another 1 to 2 teaspoons of oil to a 12- or 15-inch pizza pan (see Product List page 253) and spread it with your fingers or a pastry brush. Place the dough on the pan and shape it to fill the pan. Add your toppings. Bake the pizza on the center rack of the oven for about 20 minutes, or until done to your liking. (If baking 2 at a time, switch positions halfway through.)

▶ *After your bread or pizza dough has risen at room temperature for an hour or so, you can cover it and put it in the refrigerator to rise overnight. Then let the dough rise for 1 or 2 hours at room temperature again before shaping it. This will give you more of a sourdough than a yeasty flavor.*

Quick-Rise Pizza Dough

MAKES ENOUGH DOUGH FOR FOUR 7½-INCH MINI PIZZAS,

TWO 12-INCH THIN CRUST PIZZAS,

OR ONE THICKER CRUST 15-INCH PIZZA.

No one saves money by making homemade bread. Bakeries and supermarkets often have the same or better quality bread for virtually no more money. Baking bread is for those who love doing it. However, the money you can save making homemade pizza instead of calling for delivery can be astounding, and it doesn't really take any longer. We tested this once: My wife called for pizza delivery, and as soon as she hung up the phone, I started on this pizza dough. By the time she had handed over the $15 plus a tip for a pepperoni pizza, I was taking a homemade masterpiece out of the oven.

—WILLIAM WAGNON, Doughmakers Vice President of Marketing

4 cups all-purpose flour, plus extra for dusting if necessary
One ¼-ounce package (2¼ teaspoons) Fleischmann's Rapid Rise yeast
1½ teaspoons kosher salt
1½ cups very warm water (115°)
2 tablespoons olive oil

Place the flour, yeast, and salt in a food processor fitted with a metal blade and pulse to blend. With the machine running, slowly pour the water into the processor, then turn the machine off. Add the oil and pulse briefly to mix it in.

Turn the dough out onto a work surface and knead for about 15 strokes. The dough should be a little sticky but workable. Divide the dough into the desired number of pieces (see below). Form each piece into a ball that is roughly round or a domed disk.

At this point you may:

- Allow the dough to rest for 10 to 20 minutes while you prepare the toppings and make the pizza right away.
- Put a teaspoon of oil in a gallon-sized zippered plastic bag. Press on the outside of the bag to evenly coat with oil. Put the dough in the bag and store for a day in the

refrigerator. (The dough will continue to rise in the refrigerator, and this will give more flavor to the pizza.)

- Cover the dough tightly with plastic wrap and freeze for about 2 weeks. Remove from the freezer at least 45 minutes before using it.

▶ *Homemade pizza dough is like a blank canvas. Each pizza you make can be an opportunity for self-expression. Keep interesting ingredients on hand and try different flavor combinations.*

Sourdough Pizza Crust

MAKES TWO 12-INCH PIZZAS

SOURDOUGH STARTER:

3 cups all-purpose flour

1 tablespoon sugar

One ¼-ounce package instant yeast

2 cups very warm water (120° to 130°F)

PIZZA CRUST:

¾ cup sourdough starter (above)

2½ to 3 cups all purpose flour

1 tablespoon sugar

One ¼-ounce package instant yeast

2 teaspoons salt

¾ cup water

2 tablespoons peanut oil

Sauce of your choice

Toppings of your choice

To make the starter: Combine the flour, sugar, and yeast in a large bowl. Gradually add the water and stir until smooth. Transfer the starter to a glass or ceramic bowl or jar (not plastic). Cover it loosely with plastic or a non-airtight lid (because the fermentation process releaser gas) and let stand in a warm place until bubbly and sour-smelling, about 2 days. The starter may darken, but if it changes to another color, discard it and start over. Cover and refrigerate until ready to use.

To make the crust: Stir the sourdough starter before measuring. Measure out ¾ cup and bring to room temperature. Keep the remaining starter for later use with other recipes. In a large bowl, combine ¾ cup of flour, the sugar, yeast, and salt. Place the water and oil in a saucepan over medium heat until very warm (120° to 130°F). Gradually add this mixture and the starter to the flour mixture. Beat for 2 minutes with an electric mixer at medium speed, scraping the bowl occasionally. Stir in enough of the remaining flour to make a soft dough. Knead on a lightly floured surface until smooth and elastic, about 8 to 10 minutes. Cover the dough and let it rest for 10 minutes.

Preheat the oven to 350°F.

Divide the dough in half. Shape each half by pressing and working with your fingers to a 12-inch circle. Place on greased 12-inch pizza pans. Form a standing rim by pinching the edge of the dough. Prick the dough with a fork and let it rest for 10 minutes.

Bake for 7 minutes. Remove from the pans and cool on a wire rack until you can comfortably handle the pizzas, then add the sauce and toppings of your choice. Bake for another 10 minutes, or until the cheese, if using, is bubbly and browned. Serve warm.

▶ *Before removing your pizza from its pan or stove, check the bottom of the crust for doneness by lifting with a spatula. If it needs more time, you won't have to put it back on the pan or stove.*

Clam and Bacon Pizza

MAKES ONE 15-INCH PIZZA

We fell in love with this one at Harry's Pizzeria in West Hartford, Connecticut, and have tried our best to recreate it. Thinly sliced, it is a great appetizer pizza.

—WILLIAM WAGNON, Doughmakers Vice President of Marketing

1 recipe for Long-Rise or Quick-Rise pizza dough (pages 241 and 243)

1 to 2 tablespoons olive oil

4 strips bacon

One 4-ounce can clams

1 tablespoon grated Parmesan Cheese*

1 tablespoon grated Asiago cheese*

2 tablespoons mozzarella cheese*

Dried oregano to taste

Dried basil to taste

Dried rosemary to taste

Kosher salt to taste

Preheat the oven to 450°F. Prepare the pizza dough as directed. Shape the dough into a 15-inch pizza pan. Brush with the oil.

Place the bacon strips on a microwave-safe plate, cover loosely with a paper towel to prevent splattering, and microwave on high for 2 to 3 minutes, until about halfway done. Allow the bacon to cool, then chop it, and sprinkle it over the crust. (If you are feeling decadent, you can drizzle bacon grease from the plate onto the crust. It adds a lot of flavor.)

Drain the clams well and spread them on the pizza. Sprinkle the cheeses on top. Add the oregano, basil, rosemary, and salt to taste. Bake for 20 minutes on the bottom rack of the oven, or until lightly browned.

*You can use more than one kind of cheese, if you prefer, or different cheeses, but about ¼ cup (4 tablespoons) is appropriate.

▶ *Start a family tradition, such as pizza every Saturday night. Your children will look forward to it now and remember it as a precious memory when they are grown.*

Gorgonzola, Walnut, Pear, and Prosciutto Pizza

MAKES ONE 15-INCH PIZZA

1 clove garlic, crushed

3 to 4 tablespoons olive oil

½ recipe Long-Rise Pizza Dough
(page 241)

1 pear, peeled and thinly sliced

6 to 8 ounces Gorgonzola cheese

⅔ cup chopped walnuts toasted

4 ounces prosciutto, thinly sliced
and torn into pieces

Crush the garlic and allow it to soak in the oil for 1 hour or more.

Preheat the oven to 450°F. Prepare the pizza dough as directed. Brush a 15 inch pizza pan (see Product List, page 253) with 1 tablespoon of oil. Shape the dough and place it on the pan.

Sprinkle or brush the remaining 2 to 3 tablespoons of oil on top of the pizza dough. Arrange the pears in a single layer and add the Gorgonzola, walnuts, and prosciutto.

Bake for 15 to 20 minutes, until lightly browned.

▶ *Homemade roasted red peppers are easy to make and are a delicious addition to many pizzas. Simply place a washed red bell pepper on the grill over high heat and char the skin. Turn the pepper until it is blackened all over. Allow the pepper to cool in a brown paper bag. Under cold running water, remove the charred skin, seeds, and core.*

Grilled Chicken and Sun-Dried Tomato Pizza

MAKES ONE 15-INCH PIZZA

This colorful, tasty pizza is a good way to slip vegetables into a pizza night meal.

1 recipe for Long-Rise or Quick-Rise Pizza Dough (pages 241 and 243)

2 teaspoons olive oil

7 ounces prepared or store-bought pizza sauce

1½ to 2 cups shredded or grated mozzarella cheese

6 ounces grilled chicken breast strips (precooked strips in the grocer's frozen meat section are okay)

4 whole sun-dried tomatoes, sliced

6 ounces white button cap mushrooms, sliced

1 cup tightly packed chopped spinach leaves with stems removed

1 avocado, peeled, pitted, and sliced in strips

8 to 10 fresh basil leaves, chopped (see Tip)

Oregano to taste

Preheat the oven to 500°F.

Prepare the dough as directed. Brush a 15-inch pizza pan (see Product List, page 253) with the oil. Shape the dough and place it in the pan.

Spread a light layer of pizza sauce on the dough. Sprinkle the mozzarella cheese on the dough. Arrange the chicken strips (thawed if frozen), sun-dried tomatoes, and mushrooms. Top with the spinach, avocado, and basil. Finish with a sprinkling of oregano.

Bake for 20 minutes, or until the toppings reach desired doneness.

▶ *Bruising the basil leaves before chopping will release more flavor. Place the basil in a mortar and crush with a pestle. Or put the leaves between plastic wrap and bruise them with a meat pounder or a rolling pin.*

Onion Parmesan Flatbread

MAKES ONE 15-INCH FLATBREAD

Pizza is just another name for flatbread, which can include pita breads, focaccia (see page 106), and even tortillas and crackers. We call this "pizza" recipe a flatbread since it uses less topping than traditional pizza and the dough is made with less flour to yeast for a more bread-like result.

1 cup warm water

One ¼-ounce package active dry yeast

½ teaspoon sugar

2½ to 2¾ cups all purpose flour

1 teaspoon salt

¼ cup olive oil

1 small red onion, peeled and cut into rings

1 cup freshly grated Parmesan cheese

½ teaspoon dried rosemary

¼ teaspoon coarse salt

Pepper to taste

In a large bowl, stir together the water, yeast, and sugar. Let stand for 5 minutes, or until foamy. Stir in 2½ cups of flour and the salt until it forms a dough. Stir in the remaining flour if necessary to achieve a soft, slightly sticky, elastic dough. Knead the dough on a lightly floured surface for 5 minutes. Oil a bowl with 1 tablespoon of the oil. Add the dough to the bowl and turn to cover it with the oil. Cover the dough and let it rise in a warm place for 1 hour. Knead for 2 minutes and let rise again, covered, for 45 minutes.

Coat a 15-inch pizza pan (see Product List, page 253) with 1 tablespoon of oil. Press out the dough and stretch it to the edge of the pan. Let it rise, covered, for 1 hour. If the dough shrinks, press it to the edge again.

Sprinkle the dough with the onion and Parmesan. Drizzle with the remaining oil crumble the rosemary on top. Sprinkle with the salt and pepper. Place the flatbread on the bottom rack of a cold oven. Turn the oven to 525°F and bake for 20 to 25 minutes, or until golden and crisp.

▶ *Cut this "pizza" into small squares or long, thin slices and serve it as an appetizer before dinner.*

Carmelized Onion, Radicchio, and Goat Cheese Pizzettes

MAKES 4 INDIVIDUAL PIZZAS, OR SLICE AND SERVE AS HORS D'OEUVRES

3 tablespoons olive oil, plus additional for coating pans

1 pound red onions, thinly sliced (about 4 cups)

1½ tablespoons balsamic vinegar

2 cups chopped radicchio

Salt to taste

One Quick-Rise or ½ Long-Rise Pizza Dough (pages 241 and 243)

All-purpose flour for dusting

3 ounces goat cheese (not the soft kind), crumbled

2 teaspoons chopped fresh thyme

Preheat the oven to 500°F.

Heat the 3 tablespoons of oil in a heavy skillet and cook the onions over moderate heat until soft and a deep golden color, about 15 minutes. Remove from the heat and immediately stir in the vinegar, radicchio, and salt.

Divide the dough into quarters on a flour-dusted surface and gently press and stretch each piece into a thin disk about 8 inches across. Spread some oil on 4 mini pizza pans and place 1 disk of dough on each pan, pressing the dough to fit the pan.

Top each mini pizza with ¼ of the onion mixture, goat cheese, and thyme.

Bake the pizzas until the dough is golden, 15 to 20 minutes. Transfer to a cutting board, cut into slices, and serve immediately.

▶ *Fresh basil can be kept for up to a week if you put the sprigs in a vase with water or put the leaves in an unsealed plastic bag and store in a cool, dry place. The refrigerator is too cold. The ideal temperature is about 50°.*

Sausage, Proscuitto, and Mushroom Pizza

1 recipe Long-Rise or Quick-Rise pizza dough (pages 241 or 243)

2 teaspoons olive oil

4 ounces Italian sausage

6 ounces white button cap mushrooms, sliced

1 tablespoon butter

3 thin slices of prosciutto

7 ounces pizza sauce

1½ to 2 cups grated or shredded mozzarella cheese

1½ tablespoons pesto

Oregano to taste

Preheat the oven to 500°F.

Prepare the dough as directed. Shape the dough to fit a 15-inch pizza pan (see Product List, page 253) or other desired size that has been brushed with oil.

If using Italian sausage links, remove them from the casings. Brown the sausage in a heavy saucepan over medium-high heat for about 5 minutes. Break it up with a spoon or spatula as you go. Transfer to a plate. Drain as much fat as possible from the saucepan and sauté the mushrooms in the butter over medium high heat for 3 to 4 minutes until reduced to about half their size, then remove from the heat. Tear the prosciutto into short, thin strips.

Top the pizza crust with the pizza sauce, cheese, sausage, prosciutto, mushrooms, and pesto. Sprinkle with the oregano.

Bake for 20 minutes, or until the toppings reach the desired doneness.

▶ *Homemade pesto can be frozen in ice cube trays. Once frozen, remove them from the trays, wrap tightly in plastic, and store in the freezer. This way you can have delicious pesto in a handy quantity all through the winter.*

Product List

All of the recipes in this book can be used with your pie pans, pizza pans, muffin pans, and cookie sheets, as specified. Of course, we recommend our bakeware for the best baking results (as you know by now, we believe in what we sell!), so we've included a list of our products for your reference.

Product Name	Size
Great Grand Cookie Sheet	14" × 20½"
Grand Cookie Sheet	14" × 17½"
Biscuit Sheet	10" × 14"
Pizza Pan 15"	15" diameter
Pizza Pan 12"	12" diameter
Pizza Makers (set of 4) Mini	7½" diameter
Cake Pan 9" Round	9" diameter
Cake Pan 9" Square	9" × 9"
Cake Pan 9" × 13"	9" × 13"
Sheet Cake	13" × 18"
Jelly Roll	10" × 15"

Pie Pan with Crust Protector	9" diameter
Loaf Pan	8½" × 4½"
12-cup Regular Muffin Pan	2" cup diameter
6-cup Jumbo Muffin Pan	2¾" cup diameter
24-cup Mini Muffin Pan	3½" cup diameter
Child's Bake Set	assorted
6-piece Gift Set	assorted
12-piece Gift Set	assorted

Doughmakers® Gourmet Bakeware is available nationwide through specialty shops, gourmet stores, and select online retailers. A store locator is available at www.doughmakers.com

You can also contact us at: Doughmakers, LLC, 1650 East Industrial Drive, Terre Haute, IN 47802 (P.O. Box 10034, 47801), Phone (812) 299-8750, Toll-free (888) 386-8517, Fax (812) 299-7788.

Happy baking!

Acknowledgments

We would like to dedicate this book to our parents Jean and Howard Cuvelier. We owe our love for family and dedication to one another to the example our parents gave us. Our greatest regret is not being able to share this time and experience with Dad.

I would like to thank my husband, Brooks, our Chief Operating Officer who was willing to put everything on the line to support Diane and me in our dreams to build Doughmakers.

To our children, Emily, Tommy, Taylor, Courtney, and Daniel, thank you for your patience and willingness to help out at home and for understanding times when we were not available because of business travel and commitments. We have enjoyed many accomplishments, but you are our true masterpieces.

We want to express our love and appreciation to our other partners. We feel guilty that they do not often get to share the limelight, but without their talent and devotion, Doughmakers would not be where it is now.

To William Wagnon, our Executive Vice President of Marketing, thank you for working so hard to get Doughmakers' name out there. We know that building the brand Doughmakers has rested heavily on your shoulders, and you have accomplished something that is hard to put a value on.

To Sean McNair, our Executive Vice President of Finance, who took the burden of worrying about money and who helped us focus, stay on budget, and stretch our dollars as far as they would go, we thank you.

To Tony Buck, our Executive Vice President of Manufacturing, whose smile and warmth was always welcome, thank you for your expertise with human resources and for helping us set up disciplines to manage the business.

To our baby brother, Richard (Dicky) Cuvelier, our Executive Vice President of Sales and Marketing, who was certainly born with the gift of creativity and positive thinking. It is hard for anyone who is around you not to catch the vision and the desire to accomplish great things.

To Debbie Cuvelier, our Executive Vice President and Director of Customer Service, thank you for being the best sister-in-law, for always asking if we need help with anything, and for being willing to put in the time necessary—and always with a smile.

To Clayton (C.J.) Cuvelier, our brother and Executive Vice President and Director of Operations, thank you for your hard work ethic and your willingness to do whatever needs to be done in order to make someone else's load lighter. Also, we thank Debbie, Clay, and their three sons for having the willingness and faith in us to relocate from New York to help us.

We want to thank all our employees. You are the ones who make our wonderful product. You are the ones who work with the store and talk to our customers. You are the ones who put a face on Doughmakers and give it a personality. Each of you has contributed a part of yourself. There is no way to put a value on this. You have all become part of our family, and we have become part of yours. As we grow, we all hope to enjoy the fruit of our labors.

We have found great resources in our community and would like to acknowledge the assistance of the Rose Hulman Institute of Technology, for helping us solve problems with manufacturing; Dr. Frederica Kramer and Dr. Sarah Hawkins of the Family and Consumer Science Department of Indiana State University for helping us with research for our patent and for testing new products; Miller & White Advertising; Williams Randall Marketing Communications; and Clabber Girl.

In our journey we've had the privilege of meeting and forging relationships with many excellent people and companies in the housewares industry and food industries. For their support and encouragement, and for use of photos and recipes on our packaging (some of which appear in this book), we want to thank the following people and their companies: Keith Dierberg, Fleischmann's Yeast; Tripp Holmgrain and Belinda Ellis, White Lily Flour; Julie Ledvina, Land O' Lakes; and the members of the Home Baking Association and the Food Professionals Group. Also, we wish to thank the editors and writers at *Taste of Home*, *Cuisine at Home* (especially Sara Ostranky), *Southern Living*, *Woman's Day*, and *Fine Cooking* magazines, who received us and our products warmly. Members of the International Association of Culinary Professionals also gave us early encouragement, especially Leslie Glover Pendleton, who recruited us to join this fine association and taught us so much in two years as our spokesperson.

Many thanks to our sales representatives who introduce our products to the stores.

Last, we thank our Lord Jesus for continuing to watch over us and keeping us safe, and for giving us opportunities that we could never imagine. Although we promise to do our best as we work with others and live our lives according to His will, we often fail. Thank you for forgiveness and for the promise of a new day.

Index

Christmas clafoutis, 226
cinnamon:
    apple-banana-, muffins, 205
    rolls, overnight, 140
Clabber Girl baking powder biscuits, 99–100
Clabber Girl hot water pie crust, 220
clam and bacon pizza, 247
classic coconut cream pie, 224–25
classic pumpkin pie, 236–37
classic white bread, 97–98
Clementine's muffins, 203
cocoa, unsweetened:
    in black-and-white roulade, 147–48
    in devil's food cake, 151
    in Diane's double chocolate sheet cake, 152–53
    in double chocolate biscotti, 181–82
    in hot chocolate earthquakes, 185
    in praline turtle cake, 166–67
    see also chocolate, unsweetened
coconut:
    in Clementine's muffins, 203
    cream pie, classic, 224–25
    in gold bars, 88
    in good morning muffins, 201
    in Italian cream cake, 158–59
    in oatmeal cake, 163
    toffee bars, 84
coffee, in double chocolate biscotti, 181–82
coffee cake:
    Bev's favorite, 133
    raspberry apple, 141–42
cookies:
    Alva's spritz, 177
    best oatmeal raisin, 178
    cutouts, sugar, 190
    Denise's old-fashioned sour cream, 179
    depression, 180
    double chocolate biscotti, 181–82
    Grandma Kramer's old-fashioned sugar, 183–84
    hot chocolate earthquakes, 185
    Nancy's cheese straws, 186
    peanut butter, 194
    peanut butter oatmeal chocolate chip, 187
    pumpkin, 195
    ruskies, 193
    sealed with a kiss, 188–89
    Swedish red lips, 191
    Swedish tea cakes, 192
    see also bars
Cool Whip, in easy cut and serve cheesecake, 169
cornbread muffins, true, 204
cornmeal:
    in almond polenta cake with lemon syrup, 145–46
    in caramel pecan rolls, 135–36
    in spicy cheese muffins, 212
    in true cornbread muffins, 204
cornstarch:
    in lemon meringue pie, 232
    in raspberry apple coffee cake, 141–42
cranberry(ies):
    almond bread, 101

apple French toast bake, 137
    in orange scones, 114–15
cream, heavy:
    in almond polenta cake with lemon syrup, 145–46
    in apple bread pudding, 127–28
    in apple harvest Danish, 130
    in apple raspberry pie, 221
    in black-and-white roulade, 147–48
    in classic pumpkin pie, 236–37
    in devil's food cake, 151
    in Grandma Minnie's banana cake with whipped cream frosting, 155
    in Grandma's touch apple pie with creamy caramel sauce, 227
    in lemon chiffon pie, 231
    in maple oat scones, 139
    in pecan caramel silk pie, 234–35
    in winter wonderland bars, 89
    see also half and half
cream, light, in yule log, 172–73
cream cheese:
    in apple harvest Danish, 130
    in apple kolaches, 138
    in carrot bars, 81
    in carrot pineapple cake, 149
    in creamy apple squares, 85–86
    in easy cut and serve cheesecake, 169
    in Grandma Minnie's date nut cake, 156
    in Italian cream cake, 158–59
    in mini cheesecakes, 170
    in pecan tassies, 90
    in pumpkin cake roll, 165
    in pumpkin cookies, 195
    in raspberry apple coffee cake, 141–42
    in red velvet cake, 168
    in ruskies, 193
    in sweet rolls, 122–23
    in winter wonderland bars, 89
creamy:
    apple squares, 85–86
    caramel sauce, Grandma's touch apple pie with, 227

Danish, apple harvest, 130
date nut cake, Grandma Minnie's, 156
Denise's old-fashioned sour cream cookies, 179
depression cookies, 180
devil's food cake, 151
Diane's double chocolate sheet cake, 152–53
dill, scones, ham and, 117–18
double chocolate biscotti, 181–82
Doughmakers soft pretzels, 102–3
dreaming of New England muffins, 213

easy cut and serve cheesecake, 169
Egg Beaters, in Italian cream cake, 158–59
egg substitute:
    in Italian cream cake, 158–59
    in pecan caramel silk pie, 234–35
English bath buns, 119

evaporated milk:
   in classic pumpkin pie, 236–37
   in oatmeal cake, 163
   walnut-glazed brown sugar pound cake, 161

fennel, bacon breadsticks, 96
five-grain bread, 104–5
flatbread, onion Parmesan, 250
focaccia bread, 106–7
   blue cheese and walnuts on, 106–7
   onion and herb on, 106
   Parmesan and pecan on, 106–7
French toast bake, apple cranberry, 137
fresh blueberry banana bread, 108
fudge nut bars, 87
fudge topping, in praline turtle cake, 166–67

garlicky Parmesan and pepper dinner biscuits, 110
gelatin, in easy cut and serve cheesecake, 169
gingerbread cake with vanilla sauce, 157
goat cheese, carmelized onion, and radicchio
   pizzettes, 251
gold bars, 88
good morning muffins, 201
Gorgonzola, walnut, pear, and prosciutto pizza,
   248
graham cracker crumbs:
   in easy cut and serve cheesecake, 169
   in pecan caramel silk pie, 234–35
Grandma B's bread, 111
Grandma Klusmeier's strawberry shortcake, 109
Grandma Kramer's old-fashioned sugar cookies,
   183–84
Grandma Minnie's banana cake with whipped
   cream frosting, 155
Grandma Minnie's date nut cake, 156
Grandma Ruth's yeast rolls, 113
Grandma's touch apple pie with creamy caramel
   sauce, 227
grilled chicken and sun-dried tomato pizza, 249

half and half:
   in carmelitas, 80
   in ham and dill scones, 117–18
   in orange scones, 114–15
   see also cream, heavy
ham and dill scones, 117–18
hamburger buns, homemade, 120
herb and onion on focaccia bread, 106–7
Hershey's kisses, in sealed with a kiss cookies,
   188–89
homemade hamburger buns, 120
home-style honey wheat bread, 116
honey:
   in apple butter muffins, 207
   wheat bread, home-style, 116
hot chocolate earthquakes, 185

Italian cream cake, 158–59

jamberry pie, 229
Joyce's Texas sheet cake, 154

Karo syrup, in classic coconut cream pie, 224–25
kolaches, apple, 138

lemon:
   chess pie, 230
   chiffon pie, 231
   meringue pie, 232
   tea muffins, 210
lemon juice:
   in almond polenta cake with lemon syrup,
    145–46
   in lemon chiffon pie, 231
   in lemon meringue pie, 232
long-rise pizza dough, 241–42
   in bacon fennel breadsticks, 96

macadamia nuts, in gold bars, 88
mandarin oranges, in Clementine's muffins, 203
maple oat scones, 139
maple syrup, in dreaming of New England muffins,
   213
mascarpone cheese, in almond polenta cake with
   lemon syrup, 145–46
meringue pie, lemon, 232
mini cheesecakes, 170
molasses:
   in gingerbread cake with vanilla sauce, 157
   in sweet potato muffins, 200
mozzarella cheese:
   in grilled chicken and sun-dried tomato pizza,
    249
   in sausage, prosciutto, and mushroom pizza,
    252
muffins:
   apple-banana-cinnamon, 205
   apple butter, 207
   banana raisin oat, 206
   blackberry, 208
   blueberry, 199
   café au lait, 209
   Clementine's, 203
   dreaming of New England, 213
   good morning, 201
   lemon tea, 210
   Porter peach, 211
   ready-to-go bran, 202
   spicy cheese, 212
   sweet potato, 200
   true cornbread, 204
mushroom(s):
   in grilled chicken and sun-dried tomato pizza,
    249
   sausage, and prosciutto pizza, 252

Nancy's cheese straws, 186
Nanie's pound cake, 160
nut(s):
   in dreaming of New England muffins, 213
   fudge bars, 87
   in oatmeal cake, 163
   in ready-to-go bran muffins, 202
   see also specific nuts